BUNTING'S ANCIENT MUSIC of IRELAND

Edited from the original manuscripts
by
Donal O'Sullivan
with
Mícheál Ó Súilleabháin

CORK UNIVERSITY PRESS
1983

First published 1983 at Cork University Press
University College, Cork, Ireland.

ⓒ Cork University Press 1983
ISBN 0 902561 25 1

The Publishers gratefully acknowledge the assistance of
The Arts Council of Ireland, The Arts Council of Northern
Ireland and The National University of Ireland in making this
publication possible.

Text set in Baskerville 11 and 9 pt, by Gifford & Craven, Dublin.
Printed and bound in Ireland by Reprint Limited and
Duffy Bookbinders Limited.

ACKNOWLEDGEMENTS

I am, unfortunately, not in a position to thank the many people who were of assistance to Donal O'Sullivan in the preparation of this edition. His task of editing the texts, however, was made easier by the frequent advice of Dr. Seán Ó Súilleabháin.

In my own work, I wish to thank Professor Aloys Fleischmann for his constant encouragement and support; Professor Seán Ó Tuama for assistance with some problems relating to the Irish texts and in particular, with the list of emendations; my wife, Nóirín Ní Riain for invaluable advice on many points, and for assisting me with checking and proof-reading throughout the work. Others who made valuable detailed criticisms included Breandán Breathnach and Rev. Christopher Warren. The library staff of University College Cork, The Queen's University of Belfast, and The National Library of Ireland, should also be mentioned, as should Marian Lane for her careful and expert typing of the final manuscript; and also Coemgen Etchingham and Dónal Counihan (Cork University Press) for their patience in the final stages.

Finally I must thank the music copyist, Kevin Healy, O.S.B. of Glenstal Abbey, whose meticulous eye revealed occasional inconsistencies in the transcriptions.

None of these are, of course, responsible in any way for shortcomings in this edition.

ABBREVIATIONS

DOSB *The Bunting Collection of Irish Folk Music And Songs,* published in six parts as Volumes XXII to XXIX of the *Journal of the Irish Folk Song Society* (London, 1927 — 1939).

DOSC *Carolan, The Life, Times and Music of an Irish Harper,* two volumes (London, 1958).

1796 *A General Collection of The Ancient Irish Music,* Edward Bunting (London, n.d., [1796]).

1809 *A General Collection of The Ancient Music of Ireland,* Edward Bunting (London, 1809).

1840 *The Ancient Music of Ireland, Arranged for the Piano Forte,* Edward Bunting (Dublin, 1840).

The illustrations used within the text are taken from *The Annals of the Irish Harpers,* Charlotte Milligan Fox (London, 1911), unless otherwise indicated.

CONTENTS

LIST OF TUNE TITLES

x

FOREWORD

The completion and the editing of the late Donal O'Sullivan's work on Bunting's 1840 volume comes now as a final tribute to his labours in the field of Irish traditional music.

Perhaps some account of his career will not be out of place. Though the major part of his activities were in the political field, as Clerk of the Senate from 1922 to 1936 and Lecturer in International Affairs at TCD from 1949 to 1965, he retained all through his career an intense love of Irish folk song, derived from holidays spent as a boy with his grandparents in Kerry. So, while still a civil servant in London, he took over the editorship of the *Journal of the Irish Folk Song Society* from Mrs. Milligan Fox in 1920, and after his resignation from the Senate he devoted most of his time to research, contributing articles on Irish music and poetry to various journals, producing the booklet *Irish Folk Music and Song* (1952) for the Advisory Committee on Cultural Relations — the first general survey of the subject which was both scholarly and attractively written for the average reader — and also a lengthy and authoritative article on Irish folk music for the fifth edition of *Grove*, which included a full bibliography of the published and MS collections. His chief work followed, the monumental two-volume *Carolan — Life and Times of an Irish Harper*(1958), the first volume containing all the information available relating to Carolan and his background, with an edition of over two hundred of his airs gleaned from a wide variety of sources; the second containing exhaustive notes on the airs, biographical accounts of the patrons for whom the airs were written, and an edition of the memoirs of the harper Arthur O'Neill, a prime source for Carolan and his period. Apart from his writings, Donal O'Sullivan was an active member of the International Folk Music Council since its inception in 1947, later becoming a Vice-President. Because of his scholarly attainments and his standing generally he was awarded the honorary degree of Litt. D. by Dublin University in 1952.

While editor of the *Journal of the Irish Folk Song Society*, between 1927 and 1939 he had produced serially in the *Journal* an edition of the first two volumes of the Bunting Collection, in which the published versions were compared with Bunting's original MSS housed in the library of the Queen's University of Belfast, with the missing Irish texts restored, and with a wealth of annotations — references to further versions of the songs in other collections, and biographical notices of the traditional musicians, poets, people and place-names associated with the songs. His chief assets for this work were a sound knowledge of Irish and a photographic memory, which enabled him to trace duplicates and variants from collection to collection, and to recall interesting information in regard to almost every tune which appears in these volumes. Having completed his work on Bunting's 1809 volume in 1939, he postponed dealing with the 1840 volume to some later date, for his commitments were now becoming increasingly heavy. Concurrently with his lectureship in International Affairs at TCD, from 1951 to 1962 he held the post of Director of Studies in Irish Folk Music at UCD and on retiring from International Affairs at TCD in 1965 he was appointed Research Lecturer in Irish Folk Music. About this time he consulted Professor Boydell and myself as to which task would be the most important for him to undertake during his remaining years. We both agreed that the completion of his work on Bunting would best round off his achievements in the field of traditional music, and this advice was speedily followed. Having covered one hundred and seventeen of the tunes in the 1840 volume, however, his memory began to fail, and on his death thirty-four tunes were still unedited, while various *lacunae* in the bulk of the text remained to be filled in. The unfinished manuscript together with a collection of his books were presented by his widow, Mrs Jeannie O'Sullivan, to the Irish Folklore Department of University College, Dublin. After much deliberation the Director, Professor Almquist, decided to entrust the editing and completion of the text to Micheál Ó Súilleabháin, of the Music Department, UCC, whose publications and achievements to date clearly qualified him for the task.

He has now revised Donal O'Sullivan's text and added his own special knowledge of the collections and of the country tradition. The resultant volume is a monument, first of all to Edward Bunting himself, the pioneer who first aroused general public interest in the fast-disappearing remnants of an age-old tradition; secondly to the scholarly labours of Donal O'Sullivan, whose work would otherwise have remained incomplete; finally to the skilful editorship of Micheál Ó Súilleabháin, and to Cork University Press which has sponsored the book's publication.

Aloys Fleischmann

xiv

INTRODUCTION

This volume is the final part of Dr. Donal O'Sullivan's edition of the three Bunting collections. Parts I to VI, published between 1927 and 1939 in various issues of the *Journal of the Irish Folk Song Society*, dealt with the 1796 and 1809 collections, and this present part deals with the music in the third and final collection published in 1840.

While it was originally thought that less than one fifth of the present edition remained uncompleted, on examining the O'Sullivan manuscripts I discovered that the work was generally in an uncompleted state and needed to be revised. With few exceptions however, the words — where they were to be found — had already been edited from the Bunting manuscripts and translations added. Both translations and the text editions themselves, however, are at times questionable. Nevertheless, I wish to stress that I have not altered any of the song texts or translations in this edition with the exception of several which were left unfinished and one which escaped Donal O'Sullivan's notice in the original manuscripts. To have done so would have necessitated a completely new edition of the texts from these manuscripts. However, I have appended a short, although not complete, list of suggested emendations where this seemed most necessary.

Likewise, the majority of the tunes had been edited, although additions and corrections had to be made to about one-fifth of them. Again, over one fifth of the pieces had no notes attached, and additions have been made to the remainder. An Appendix has also been added by me dealing with the tunes found in the Preface and Introduction to Bunting's *1840* volume. It should be noted that in attempting to alter as little as possible of the notes written by Donal O'Sullivan to the pieces, I have retained his use of the first person singular when it occurs. Any additions made by me to the Notes, however, have been clearly marked in square brackets. A Bibliography has also been added, as have various Indexes in line with those in the earlier editions.

While the general lay-out and approach of this edition is much the same as the earlier ones, it differs in two basic respects. Firstly, editorial notes, involving a detailed commentary on the changes made in editing the tunes, have been omitted by Donal O'Sullivan from under the music. Secondly, the words of the songs have not been set to the music. To do this properly would mean re-editing the tunes specially for the purpose and would require a separate work.

The words to less than a third of the tunes in the *1840* volume have been found in the Bunting manuscripts. Also, the original sketches of about one-fifth of the tunes have not been found. It should be mentioned here, however, that MSS 13 and 27, being a final fair copy of the music (including piano accompaniment) before publication, contain nearly all the tunes. Since these versions are usually identical with the published version, they have not been mentioned in the notes, unless for some particular reason.

The introductory section to Donal O'Sullivan's earlier Bunting editions contains an essay entitled "A short account of Bunting as Collector", dealing mainly with historical and biographical detail. The notes to the present edition (and, in particular, my own additions) touch at times on Bunting as collector from a purely musical point of view (see, for example, the notes to Numbers 1, 3, 30, 37, 46, 78, 89, 139). In these cases, and in others, a comparison between manuscript and published versions of tunes show Bunting to have adopted a somewhat less scientific approach to his work than one might be inclined to believe from the general tenor of his own notes. While preparing the tunes for publication, he obviously found himself presented with a musical idiom, even in his own notebooks, not wholly in keeping with his musical understanding. On top of this, the task of adding piano accompaniments must have quickly brought to the surface those sometimes subtle, but always important ingredients, which separated the Irish harping tradition from the main body of European Art music of the times as a unified *genre*. Matters such as asymmetrical phrase lengths, variable notes, gapped scales, the modal nature of the music, and at times even the characteristic melodic movement of the pieces, caused him to have second thoughts at publication stage. The conflict can be seen to surface in "Scots Lamentation, with the original bass and treble, as played by Hempson, precisely as he learnt it from Bridget O'Cahan," where Bunting prints two versions of the piece: the first, in all probability, his sincere attempt at capturing Hempson's performance on paper; the second, his elaboration of the piece for piano in line with his own musical expectations and those of his average reader (see notes to tune No. 8).

On the negative side, therefore, we can see how Bunting knocked the attractive edges from some of the tunes and neatly rounded the phrases (e.g. No. 1 and No. 30). Many pieces were forced into major and minor keys and appropriate accidentals were introduced (e.g. No. 3). Heavy handed accompaniments were added (although these may contain traces of the original harper's 'accompaniment', e.g. see No. 43) and, in some cases, tunes which show themselves to be full of interest and life in the original sketches, lose a great deal of their impact and distinctiveness in their published form. Nevertheless, any balanced overall evaluation of Bunting as collector will result in a positive reaction to his life's work, particularly when viewed in the context of his time and of the musical wealth of his manuscripts. If these had never surfaced, we would today still rejoice in his published work. The survival of the manuscripts, however, allows us to investigate his weakness as editor, while appreciating his initial drive and strength as collector.

As to the present edition, while certain elements in Donal O'Sullivan's approach may be seen to be idiosyncratic from the viewpoint of contemporary scholarship in traditional music studies, nevertheless the scope and consistency of his research has contributed towards making such publications as his earlier Bunting editions, and his Carolan edition, standard works of reference. The Bunting manuscripts, however, have yet to reveal a great deal of information. Quite apart from the material which remains unpublished, purely musical aspects of the published pieces, such as the harp basses (Nos. 8, 43, 156), or the variations "in the old Irish style" (*1840* Preface, p.9), were sometimes overlooked by Donal O'Sullivan in his efforts to investigate the historical background to the pieces. Likewise, Bunting's *1840* volume contains several introductory chapters (the most important being entitled 'Of the method of playing and musical vocabulary of the old Irish harpers') and these have not fallen within the scope of the present edition.

My own task of editing Donal O'Sullivan's uncompleted edition of Bunting's edition of his own manuscripts, has had its own complexities. In all of this, I have endeavoured to follow the original intentions and usual practice of Donal O'Sullivan as conscientiously as possible, and my hope is that this volume will serve to complement the earlier Bunting editions by bringing to fruition his original ideal of a complete edition of Bunting's volumes.

Micheál Ó Súilleabháin

1. SUIDH SÍOS FÁ MO DHÍDEAN
Sit Down Under My Protection

TITLE: *1840, p.I:* Sit down under my protection. Index, p.VI: Suidh sios ar mo dhidion. Tune: MS.33, Bk.4, p.6 — "Shios ar mo dhidion".

NOTES

Taken down by Bunting from Charles Byrne in 1799. Though played by Byrne on the harp, this is a song air. But the words are not in the Bunting MSS., and I have failed to find them elsewhere. [The air also appears in MS.33, Book 5, p.1, in the key of three flats with a bass accompaniment and marked "Andante". It was probably copied from MS.33, Bk.4, p.6, with the bass added. Bunting's treatment of this piece in the *1840* publication is a clear example of how he would alter those tunes which contained characteristics at variance with his musical training and understanding. The air as he collected it can be seen to have its first part made up of one four-bar phrase and two three-bar phrases. In the *1840* publication we find this altered to three regular four-bar phrases. The second part of the air he treats in a similar fashion.]

1

2. LADY IVEAGH

TITLE: *1840, p. 2:* Lady Iveach. Index p.II: Bantiarna Ibheachadh. Tune: MS. 33, Bk. 2, p.42 — "Bantighearna Ibheach — Lady Iveagh".

NOTES

This is a harp version of a song air, the words of which have not survived. It was obtained by Bunting from Arthur O'Neill in 1792. On p.IX of the Index Thomas Connallon is named as the composer, but the Introduction (p.70) attritubes it to Connallon's younger brother William. Thomas was born at Cloonmahon, County Sligo in 1640 and his brother five years later (pp.69-70).

Bunting's comment (p.91) is as follows: "An air remarkable for its haughty and majestic style, suitable most probably to the rank and character of the lady to whom it is addressed. The Lady Iveagh whose name is preserved in this characteristic melody was Sarah, daughter of Hugh O'Neill, the great Earl of Tyrone. She was married to Art Roe Magennis [Aodh Ruadh Mag Aonghuis], who was created Viscount Iveagh by patent of July 18th, 1623."

Iveagh is a barony in County Down, and most of the land was granted by Queen Elizabeth in 1584 to the Magennis family, who had been lords of the territory for centuries. The name is now commonly called Guinness, and particulars of the lords of Iveagh are given in the *Complete Peerage*, 1932 edition pp.349-354. Arthur Magennis married Sarah O'Neill before the 4th March, 1594-5.

She became the first Lady Iveagh when her husband was raised to the peerage in 1623 and she died in 1644, having survived her husband by fifteen years. Hence she was not a contemporary of the Connellans, and if the air was composed by either of them she cannot be the subject. It must be by some unknown musician.

On the other hand, if it is a Connellan composition the probable subject is the last Lady Iveagh. The dynasty created by the Stuarts was Catholic, and it came to an end when the fifth Viscount, who was a nephew of the first and succeeded in 1684, was attainted by William of Orange in 1691. Two years earlier he had married Margaret, daughter of the seventh Earl of Clanricarde, who accompanied her husband when he accepted military service under the Emperor of Austria. On his death in Hungary in 1692 she returned to Ireland and married in 1696 Colonel Thomas Butler of Kilcash, dying a widow in 1744. During the brief period when she was Lady Iveagh the brothers Connallon were in their forties. She is said to have been a lady of great personal charm; and in his *Irish Minstrelsy* (1831), Vol 2, p.266, Hardiman published a long ode in Irish, stated in the notes (p.417) to have been written in her praise by "a grateful student of the name of Lane, whom this excellent woman had educated, at her own expense, for the priesthood".

Kilcash, where Lady Iveagh lived from her second marriage until her death, is a small country village about six miles east of Clonmel, County Tipperary; but the seat of the Butlers of Ormonde has long disappeared. By 1800 it had become a ruin, and according to a note in *Castlehaven's Memoirs* (1815), p.23, the remains were sold by the then Lord Ormonde for a trifling sum. Not long before that, the condition of this once great country seat was described in a touching poem by an unknown writer, entitled "Caoine Chille Cais" (Lament for Kilcash). Its seven verses contain several allusions to Lady Iveagh, and she is mentioned by name in one of them — which suggests that among the people of that locality she was still known by her former title after her second marriage. The Lament is printed in Edward Walsh's *Poets and Poetry of Munster* (1840), pp.196-202. It will be sufficient to quote the first two verses. The cutting down of the trees, mentioned in the second line, was done by the forces of William of Orange to prevent the Irish soldiery from sheltering in them. The English verse-rendering is so well done that I give it instead of a prose translation

Cad a dhéanfamíd feasta gan adhmad?
    Tá deire na gcoillte ar lár.
Níl trácht ar Chill Cais ná a teaghlach,
    'S ní bainfear a cling go bráth:
An áit úd 'ná gcomhnuigheadh an deigh-bhean
Fuair gradaim is meidhir tar mnáibh,
Bhíodh Iarlí a' tarraign tar tuínn ann,
    'S an tAifreann doimhinn dá rádh.

Is é mo chreach fhada 's mo léan-ghoirt
Do gheataí breágha néata ar lár!
An *Avenue* ghreanta faoi shaothar,
 'S gan fosg' ar aon taobh do'n *Walk*!
An Chúirt bhreagh a' sileadh an braon di,
 'S an gasradh séimh go tláth,
'S an leabhar na marbh do léightar
An tÉasbog 's an Lady Iveágh!

TRANSLATION

Oh, sorrow the saddest and sorest!
 Kilcash's attractions are fled —
Felled lie the high trees of its forest,
 And its bells hang silent and dead.
There dwelt the fair lady, the vaunted,
 Who spread through the island her fame,
There the Mass and the Vespers were chaunted,
 And thither the proud Earls came!

I am worn by an anguish unspoken
 As I gaze on its glories defaced,
Its beautiful gates lying broken,
 Its gardens all desert and waste.
Its courts, that in lightning and thunder
 Stood firm, are alas! all decayed,
And the Lady Iveagh sleepeth under
 The sod, in the greenwood shade.

The last two lines depart somewhat from the original, which means:
"And in the Book of the Dead one may read (the names of) the
Bishop and Lady Iveagh". The former was Bishop Butler of West-
Court, Callan, brother of Lady Iveagh's second husband. It should
also be mentioned that, in Irish, "Iveagh" is a spondee — two equal
syllables, and is prounced "Eve-awe."

[There is a very rough second copy of the tune to be found in
MS.33, Bk.5, p.53. It is in the key of C and has the title "Lady
Iveagh in her silk brocade dress sailing about" and is marked "Pom-
poso". In MS.33, Bk.4, p.71, there is a tune called "Miss Crofton",
which is a variant of "Lady Iveagh." The origin or composer is not
stated. In *DOSC* II, pp.19/20 'Miss Crofton' is attributed to Carolan
on the assumption that it is written in his style.]

4

3. THE BLACKBIRD AND THE THRUSH

TITLE: *1840, p.3:* The blackbird and the thrush. Tune: MS.29, p.91 — no key or time signature. A rough copy. "An londubh agus an ciarseach — The blackbird and the thrush".

TRANSLATION

One evening as I walked down by yon green bush,
I heard two birds whistling, 'twas the blackbird and the thrush.
I asked them the reason they were so merrie,
And the answer that they gave me, they were single and free.

I sent my love a red rose, a red rose so fine,
She sent me back an answer, mixed with rue and thyme,
Saying, "Keep you your red rose and I'll keep my thyme,
And drink to your true love, and I'll drink to mine."

I sent my love a letter to see if she'd mourn,
She sent back an answer, she could do her own turn:
"I can work or sit idle, if occasion I see,
I can rest when I'm tired, he is no match for me."

Oh! meeting's a pleasure, but parting's a grief,
And an inconstant lover is worse than a thief.
For a thief can but rob you, steal all that you have,
But an inconstant lover would send you to your grave.

NOTES

AIR: [There is a fair copy in MS.33, Bk.3, p.40, marked "Tempo di Minuetto", on which Bunting has written "From Charles Byrne's singing". But in the Index he states that it was obtained "at Ballinrobe, Co. Mayo, 1792". Both the printed tune and the fair copy differ from the rough copy, edited above, on account of the D sharp and E sharp included by Bunting.]

WORDS: None in these MSS. But those given above, which are appropriate to the tune, were learnt by Miss Honoria Galwey "from a servant in the County Derry" in 1864 who sang them to a different tune. The words were printed in the *Journal of the Irish Folk Song Society*, Vol. IV (1906), p.33; and both words and tune were published in Miss Galwey's book *Old Irish Croonauns* (1911), p.12 and 31.

4. WHISH, CAT FROM UNDER THE TABLE

TITLE: *1840, p.3:* Huish the cat. Index, p.IV: Huis an cat. Tune: MS.33, Bk.2, p.69: "Whish, cat, from under the table".

NOTES

Noted from Charles Byrne in 1802. The only words are the two opening lines, which are given with the music, as follows:

Whish, cat, from under the table,
And you shall have milk while ever I'm able.

The air "Katty Quin", No.88 *infra*, is a close variant.

[There is an identical copy of this tune with the same title in MS.33, Bk.5, p.48.

The copy in O'Neill's *Music of Ireland* No.909 is probably taken from Bunting. "Dance light, for my heart lies under your feet" is given as an alternative title. Roche's *Collection of Irish Airs, Marches and Dance Tunes*, Vol. 3, p.5, No.114, entitled "Hunt the Cat," is a variant of the Bunting tune. Another variant is to be found on Tape No.22B in the tape archive of the Music Department, University College, Cork. This field-recording of the singing and accordian playing of Conchubhar Ó Laoghaire (Doire 'n Chuilinn, Cúil Aodha, Co. Cork) was made by Máire Ní Luasa in 1979 and contains a dance tune entitled "Wallop the Cat" with the following verse which the performer learnt from his father and grandmother.

Wallop the cat, he's fine and he's fat,
Wallop the cat from under the table.
Wallop the cat, he's fine and fat,
Wallop the cat from under the table.

In the notes to tunes No.39 and 49 in *Ceol Rinnce na hÉireann*, Vol.2, pp.165/66, Breandán Breathnach mentions the Bunting tune in connection with a number of other jig-tunes, in particular "Bímid Ag Ól". There are also motivic connections with a reel, "Gilibeart Mhac Fhlannchadha" in *Ceol Rinnce na hÉireann*, Vol.1, No.83, and with a slip-jig, "Last Night's Fun" in Vol.2, No.107. Another variant entitled "Jackson's Humours of Panteen" is ascribed to the 18th century piper, Walker Jackson and occurs in Lee's *Jackson's Celebrated Irish Tunes*, p.3.]

5. AN CEANNAIDHE SÚGACH
The Jolly Pedlar

TITLE: *1840, p.4:* The merchant's daughter. Index, p.I: An ceannaidhe sugach. Index, p.XI: The jolly merchant. Tune: MS.33, Bk.5, on a loose page pinned between pp.48 and 49: "Cannae sugah. The merry merchant's daughter." It lacks the two final bars, which were evidently on a missing page.

NOTES

This piece was taken down from Kate Martin, County Cavan, in 1802. Bunting's English title is hopelessly wrong. "Daughter" does not occur at all in the original. The word *ceannaidhe* means literally "buyer", but when Irish was generally spoken it came to mean a person who buys and sells: what we should call a dealer or, if on a larger scale, a merchant. Folk tunes come from rural localities, not from towns, and I have personally no doubt that "An Ceannaidhe Súgach" means "The Jolly Pedlar." Similarly, the eighteenth century Munster poet Andrew MacGrath (whose verse was edited by the Rev. P.S. Dinneen) was popularly known as "An Mangaire Súgach", which means exactly the same thing.

[Although both the MS. copy and the published version of this tune contain a raised 7th and a raised 4th, there can be little doubt that this was orginally an aeolian tune.]

6. AN bhFACA TÚ AN STARRAIDHE DUBH?
Did you see the Dark-haired Playboy?

TITLE: *1840, p.4:* Did you see the Black Rogue. Index, p.I: An bhfeacadh tu an stadhaire dubh. Tune: MS.33, Bk.2, p.57: "Bhacca dubh en starrae dubh gera'm mna". This should read: "An bhfeacadh tú an starraidhe dubh ag iarraidh mná?" meaning "Did you see the dark haired playboy looking for a wife? — or "for a woman?".

8

NOTES

This tune, the words of which have not survived, was noted from
Hugh Higgins in 1792, according to the Index. But in the MS.
original the following was written underneath the tune: "From Arthur O'Neill and also from an old Printed Collection." The tune
had already appeared in Holden's *Collection of old Established
Irish slow and quick Tunes*, Vol. II (1806), p.7: "Have you seen my
black deceiver?" and Mulholland's *Ancient Irish Airs* (1810), p.66:
"A staraidh dubh – The Black Jester."

[This tune is also found in Neale's *Celebrated Irish Tunes* (c. 1726)
p.17.]

7. AN LONDUBH AGUS AN CHÉIRSEACH
The Blackbird and the Woodlark

TITLE: *1840, p.5:* The Blackbird and the Hen. Index, p.II: An Londubh agus
an Cheirseach. Tune: MS.33, Bk.2, p.37 — "Cearc is Coileach. The Cock and
Hen."

Tá'n londubh 's an chéirseach 's an *nightingale* le chéile,
'S an smóilín binn bréagach 'n-a ndéigh in gach áird,
An chuach imeasc an méid sin a' seinim dán is dréachta
Do chúl trom deas na bpéarlaí is dom' chéad míle grádh

Dá mbeinnse féin 'mo smóilín leanfainn tríd a' mhóin í,
Mar 'bhfuil sí bláth na h-óige, 'sí thóigeadh suas mo chroidhe;
Bheinn a' sinim ceóil dí ó mhaidin go tráthnóna,
Le ceiliúr binn dá cealgadh 's le mórdháil dá sgiamh.

Is truagh gan mé, 'mo shiúirín is barr mo ghéaga dlúth léi,
Go seinnfinn dí go súgach ar chiúl-chruit go sámh.
A laoigh, narbh' aoibhinn domh-sa dá bhfuighinn cead bheith 'siubhal léi,
'S a rún mo chroide bí 'súil liom le h-éirghe dhon lá.

TRANSLATION

1. The blackbird and the woodlark and the nightingale are together, And the tuneful deceitful little thrush after them in every direction. The cuckoo in the midst of them singing lays and songs To the beautiful abundant locks of the fair one and to my hundred thousand loves. 2. If I were myself a little thrush I would follow her through the mountain bog, For she is the blossom of youth, 'tis she who used to lift up my heart; I would play music to her from morning till evening, Winning her with sweet melody, and with delight in her beauty. 3. 'Tis a pity I am not a sweetheart(?) with my arms around her, So that I might play to her happily on a harp in tranquil mood. Beloved, how happy I should be if I had leave to walk with her, And, darling of my heart, be expecting me at day-break.

NOTES

According to the Index, the tune was noted at Ballinrobe, County Mayo, in 1792. The words are in MS.7, No.139 and are from the same county. The first two verses are "from John Gaven, Drummin, eight miles south of Westport" in 1802, and the third from "blind Redmond Stanton of Westport" in the same year.

[A version of the words is also in Hyde's *Abhráin Ghrádha Chúige Chonnacht* p.95/96. There is a related tune in Petrie's *Ancient Music of Ireland* (1855) p.162 under the title "Cearc agus Coileach a d'imigh le chéile." Also, "Sweet Portaferry", No. 76 in this edition is related.]

10

8. SCOTT'S LAMENTATION FOR THE BARON OF LOUGHMOE

TITLE: *1840, p.6:* Scott's Lamentation for the Baron of Loughmoe — in 1599 Index, p.III: Cumha caoine an Albanaigh — Scott's Lamentation. Tune: MS.33, Bk.2, p.17: "Denis Hempson — This is one of the Old Irish Lessons for the harp".

NOTES

Bunting states (p.69) that the composer of this air was John Scott, a sixteenth century harper who was a native of the county of Westmeath. According to the above MS., the subject was *"Thomas Purcell,* styled in his will Baron of Loughmoe (will dated 26th March, 1597), who died 3rd August, 1607. He married Jeanna Fitzpatrick and had 5 sons and 5 daughters. We have a record of 5 generations of his descendants". Here he appears to be quoting from the material in the Office of Arms (now the Geneaological Office), Dublin Castle. On p.90 he gives the year of death as "about A.D. 1599" and adds: "The Purcells were at this time a family of great consideration in the midland counties; they were allied to the Fitzpatricks, Earls of Upper Ossory, and had six castles in the County of Kilkenny."

The *Complete Peerage* mentions no Barony of Loughmoe, and the name does not occur in the *Index of Townlands.* As to the Fitzpatricks, they were Barons, not Earls. Brian MacGiolla Phádraig (Brian Kilpatrick) was created Baron of Upper Ossory by Henry VIII in 1541. He died in 1575 and was succeeded by his eldest son, also named Brian. The Jeanna Fitzpatrick mentioned above may have been one of the daughters of the second Baron.

[There is a rough copy of the piece in MS.29, pp.156-158 with no key or time signature and with no bass. A second rough copy, with a bass, is in MS.33, Bk.5, No.75.

Bunting prints another version of the piece, with a different bass, in the Introduction to the *1840* volume facing p.89 with the following note on p.89: "Scott's Lamentation — with the original bass and treble, as played by Hempson, precisely as he learned it from Bridget O'Cahan. This specimen probably belongs to that highly finished school of performance which so much excited the admiration of Giraldus in the twelfth century." The version in the Introduction is entitled "Scott's Lamentation, as originally performed by Hempson on the Irish harp." The bass here is interesting as compared with the more elaborate and predictable arrangement by Bunting of the version in the main body of the book, p.6. The texture is sparse with mostly octave doublings except for occasional full chords at cadential points. The erratic 'pointing' of the treble by the bass is reminiscent of the fragmented lower octave doublings of the melody in some examples of contemporary Irish traditional concertina playing where this technique lends a sense of urgency to the music. At any rate, it is probable that the notation in MS. 33, Bk.5, No.75 is a later attempt by Bunting to capture the piece on paper, with the MS.29 notation and his own memory as his only aids.

On pp. 90/91 of the Introduction, Bunting writes: "The Caoine was a solemn piece of music, intended as a tribute of respect to the deceased, and was looked on as the greatest test of the abilities of the harper. It consisted of three divisions in one lesson and was not intended to be sung. It will be observed that throughout this piece, the arrangement of which certainly exhibits a vast deal of art and energy, the fourth tone of the diatonic scale never once occurs."

Bunting goes on to attribute the hexatonic nature of the tune to "the fashion of the time; an explanation supported very strongly by the fact, that in all Rory Dall O'Cahan's pieces composed very shortly after, the tone of the subdominant or fourth is studiously avoided".]

9. LADY MAISTERTON

TITLE: *1840, p.8:* The Wood Hill or Lady Maisterton. Index, p.III: Cnoc na Coille. Tune: MS.33, Bk.3, p.62: "Lady Maisterton very ancient. From Martin a harpress in County Cavan".

NOTES

[According to Bunting's printed index, the tune was noted from "C. Martin, harper at Virginia, 1800".

Another copy, scribbled and incomplete, is in MS.29, p.204. The title given is "Lady Maisterton" and the original of the tune is not stated. The alternative title does not appear on the MS.]

The name "Maisterton" is Scottish and there is no record of it in the Irish peerage or baronetage, or in the Genealogical Office in Dublin Castle.

The *Index of Townlands* places "Woodhill or Knocknakillew" (Cnoc na Coille) in County Sligo, and it is possible that people named Maisterton lived there. But there is no mention of them in the two standard histories of Sligo by Wood, Martin and O'Rourke.

10. UCH NA n-UCH IS OSNA I LÁR MO CHLÉIBH
Alas and alas and a sigh in the depth of my breast!

TITLE: *1840, p.9:* Alas the pain in my heart. Index, p.VI: Uch nan uach is osna lar mo cleibh. Tune: MS.33, Bk.I, p.I. "Uch nan oh! is osna lar mo chliabh". "Alas alas! the pain in my heart".

14

WORDS: MS.7, No.63

Uch na n-uch is osna i lár mo chléibh!
Tá mo cháirde anocht ag moladh mná dhom féin.
Ní thiubhrainn toil don chrodh nach fearrde mé,
Go n-ólfainn deoch gan locht le grádh geal mo chléibh!

A cháirde gaoil, Ó caoinidh m'ádhbhar féin,
Bheigh ceangailte le mnaoi 's gan m'intinn sásta léi,
Mar gheall ar mhaoin beag saoghalta nach fearrde mé —
Trí ba, caoire 'gus siabhradh mná gan chéill.

Bhí mé lá 's ba mhór mo ghrádh 's mo ghean,
Is bhéaradh mná óga póga is fáilte dhom.
Tiacht a' Domhnaigh ba mhór mo stáid as sin,
Is féach mar chuaidh an pósadh gránda sin dúinn!

Grádh mo chroidhe do chionn, do chiabh 's do rosg,
'S do bhéilin binn nár chuimhrigh ariamh ar an olc,
Do dhá chích cruinn mar thuinn a d'éirochadh ar loch,
'S nach brúighte tinn mé ag ionnsuidhe an tsléibhe so anocht!

TRANSLATION

1. Alas and alas and a sigh in the depth of my breast! My friends to-night are commending a woman to me. I would not be minded for wealth when I should not be the better of it, But I would readily drink a drop with the bright love of my breast! 2. Dearest friends, O! pity my case, To be bound to a woman when my mind is not satisfied with her. On account of a few wordly goods that I am not the better of — Three cows, sheep and a ghastly woman without intellect. 3. There once was a time when my love and affection stood high, And young women would give me kisses and welcome. When Sunday came, great was my standing on that account, And look how this hateful marriage has worked out for me! 4. My heart's love are your head, your tresses and your eyes, And your sweet little mouth that never even thought of anything evil, Your two round breasts like waves rising on a lake, And how bruised and ill I am as I make for the mountain to-night!

15

NOTES

The tune was noted from Charles Byrne in 1792. The source of the words is given as McDermot, a shoemaker in Castlebar. The MS. version is in rough notation.

[The title of this piece is also the opening line of one of the many versions of the song "Casadh An tSúgáin" which is dealt with in *DOSB* I p.65.]

11. CONCHUBHAR MHAC COIRÉIBHE
Conor Macareavy

TITLE: *1840, p.10:* Conor Macareavy. Index, p.III: Conchobhar Macaraibhe.
Tune: MS.5, p.20.

WORDS: MS.6, p.63.

A Chnochúir, a Chnochúir, a Chnochúir 'ac Coiréibhe,
Buin a' chluig ins a' ghoirt agus déanamuíd réidhteach.
Buin a' cheann den neóinín, 'sé an treóiruidhe beag tréith-lag,
Bobarú, 'Dhiarmuidín, is d'éaluigh mé 'réir leat.

Tá aon beag muilid mar dhrilin tríd bháine a ghruaidh,
I gceann gach tubaiste ag imirt in' chlár go buan.
A bhaill cheart mhilis, ná leig-se go bráth mé uait,
'S gur crann gan duilliúr an duine gan grádh gan fuath.

16

Tá mé lag claoidhte 's gan brigh in mo bhallaibh,
Gan eallach, gan maoin, gan spré ar a'talamh.
Bím buidheach do Dhia 's mo shaoghal iar n-a chaitheamh,
Mo dhíomas dhá chlaoidh 's mé arís i mo leanbh.

TRANSLATION

1. Conor, Conor, Conor Macareavy, Pluck the bluebell in the field and let us make peace, Pluck the head from the daisy, 'tis a weak little guide, Bobaro, little Dermot, I eloped with you yestreen. 2. There's a little ace of diamonds sparkling through the white, And the worst of it is, bad luck always plays on my table. O dear sweet companion, never part from me till death, And like a leafless tree is a man without love or hate. 3. I am worn out and weak, without strength in my limbs, Without cattle, without wealth, without a dowry on earth. I'm thankful to God that my life is near its end, That my pride is subdued and that I am again a child.

NOTES

AIR: As printed in *1840*, the tune is very different from that in the MS. It is followed by three extensive "variations" (which are not in the MSS.) said to be composed by Lyons in 1700, and the notation is from Hempson at Magilligan in 1792. Another copy, similar but not identical, is in MS.6, p.53.

On p.98, Bunting states that the tune is also known by the name "A chailíní, an bhfaca sibh Seoirse?" (Girls, have you seen George?) which is printed in his *1796 Collection* as tune No. 6 (cf. *DOSB* I, 6). [In one of the two MS. versions of the tune under the latter title (MS.29, p.32) an examination of the third section (i.e. bar 17 to the end) shows it to be related to Variation No.2 (*1840, p.II*). In the same MS. Bunting states that "McCabe's verses of Carolan (are) to the same tune". This is an obvious reference to yet another version of the tune under a third title: "Sgarúint na gCompánach" (The Parting of Friends) which appears as tune No.25 in the *1796 Collection* by Bunting. However, Bunting's note is an error in that Carolan's verse on McCabe — not vice versa — are sung to this tune. The tune is also found in Neal's *Celebrated Irish Tunes* (c. 1726) p.18 and in Mulholland's *Ancient Irish Airs* (c. 1810) No.36.]

In Walker's *Irish Bards* Vol. I, p.320, it is stated that Carolan's elegy on the death of his wife, Mary Maguire, was written to it. This is probably enough, as the meter is the same. Incidentally, the elegy is one of Carolan's best poems.

12. THE ROSE WITHOUT RUE

TITLE: *1840, p.12, No.12:* The Rose without rue. Index: no Irish title given. Tune: *1840,* p.12.

NOTES
There is no MS. copy. According to the Index of *1840*, p.V, the tune was noted at Coleraine, County Londonderry in 1810.

13. SEABHAC NA h-ÉIRNE
The Hawk of Ballyshannon

TITLE: *1840, p.13:* The Hawk of Ballyshannon. Index, p.V: Seabhac na h-Eirne. Tune: MS.33, Bk.3, p.10. "Seabhac na hEirne or Hawk of Lough Erne or Miss Moore. From Arthur O'Neill — with words Irish and English by Carolan."

Ag so féirín deagh-mhná is áille
Ó Chonar Uí Raghallaigh go Sléibhtibh Uí Mháille.
An rígh-bhean óg is milse póg,
Ar Inghin Uí Mhórdha a thráchtaim;
Gaol na mbrígh-bhfear láidir,
Is faide a léigheadh cíos ar cáirde,
Plannda an tséin is na réidh-bhfolt daithte,
Is tú atáim a' rádh anois.

Nárbh aoibhinn don té a bheith dá caidreadh,
Géag na gcuachal fáinneach,
Siúr na righthe aníos ó Theamhair,
Shíolruigh ó Chonall Cheárnach.
Molaim thú féin an réim so a ghlacadh,
Aon-mhic tapuidhe Mhánuis,
Seabhac na h-Éirne is Bhéal Atha Seanaidh,
Is mian croidhe gach óig-mhná.

TRANSLATION
1. Here is a gift of the fairest of women From Conor O'Reilly to the Mailey hills, The queenly young woman whose kiss is sweetest, It is of O'More's daughter that I speak: Kinswoman of men vigorous and powerful, Who would never accept rent from their friends, Scion of good fortune of the smooth bright locks, 'Tis you that I now mention. 2. How happy would be the one who caressed her, Young lass of the ringletted locks, Descendant of the ancient kings of Tara. Of the seed of Conal Carnach: I applaud you for taking this course, Dexterous only son of Manus, Hawk of the Erne and of Ballyshannon, Heart-throb of every young woman.

NOTES
AIR: Noted by Bunting from Arthur O'Neill in 1792.

[There is another copy in MS.33, Bk.5, pp.31a — 31b: "Seabhac na Heirne. The Hawk of Lough Eirne of Ballyshannon".]
    In his Introduction to the *1840* volume, p.91, Bunting states that the air is "an altered composition of Rory Dall, being his "Port Atholl" somewhat varied by Carolan". All that is known of this harper is given in Part VI of my Bunting Collection pp.42-49. His precise dates are unknown, but his period is roughly 1550-1650. He was a member of a noble family of County Derry and lived chiefly in Scotland, where he composed tunes called 'ports', for the Scottish nobility, of which "Port Atholl" is one.
    As Bunting states, it was adapted by Carolan; and the resulting song, as the above verses indicated, celebrates the marriage of Charles O'Donnell, son of Colonel Manus O'Donnell of Newport, County Mayo, to Katherine O'More, daughter of Colonel Lewis O'More, who lived at Ballyna House, Moyvalley, County Kildare. Both families belonged to the Irish Catholic gentry and suffered by the Penal Laws. The date of the marriage is not given, but Charles O'Donnell died in 1770 (cf. *DOSC* II, p.82).

[Joyce prints the tune in his *Old Irish Folk Music and Songs*, p.298.]

WORDS: The first two of eight stanzas printed in Thaddaeus Connellan's *An Duanire (Fonna Seanma)* (1829): reprinted in my edition of Carolan, I, p.235 ("Katherine O'More"), with words and notes in II, pp.82-85. No English words (as mentioned in MS.33, bk.3, p.10) are extant.

14. ROSEY CONNOLLY

TITLE: *1840, p.14* Rose Connolly. Index: p.V. Róisín Ní Chonilláin. Tune: MS.33, Bk.5, p.32: "Rosey Connolly", with the following verse on p.33:

All you young men and Maidens I pray you take warning by me,
And never court your true love anunder a Hozier Tree.
The devil and his temptations it was that came over me,
And I murdered my Rosey Connolly anunder a Hozier Tree.

NOTES

AIR: The Index states that the tune was noted at Coleraine in 1811.
WORDS: The word "Hozier" is not in the Oxford Dictionary. Presumably the ozier is meant — a form of willow. The word "anunder" is strange. [In *Irish Folk Music*, p.129, O'Neill mentions a ballad called "The Fair at Dungarvan" as being sung to a variant of Bunting's tune.]

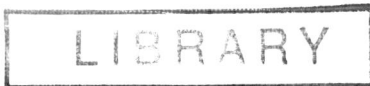
21

15. AR A' mBAILE SEO TÁ AN CHÚILFHIONN
In this village dwells the fair lady

TITLE: *1840, p.14:* In this village there lives a fair maid. Index, p.I: Air an m-baile so ta cuilfhionn. Tune: MS.33, Bk.5, p.29. "Erigh Maully Shaugh Coolin. In this village lives a fair maid".

WORDS: MS.7, No.156

Ar a' mbaile seo tá an chúlfhionn 's a' mhaighre bhreágh mhúinte,
'Sí an buinneán is úire í dá bhfaca mé do mhnáibh,
'Sí mo shearc í, 'sí mo rún í, 'sí bláth na n-úbhall cúmhra í,
'Sí an samhra 'san fhuacht í, eidir Nodlaic is Cáisc.

Is aoibhinn don chéarsaigh a mbíonn an londubh dhá bréagadh,
Mar islighid re chéile faoi'n aon-chraobh amháin.
Ní h-é sin domh-sa le mo chéad-searc, is fada ghabhamaoid ón sgéal sin,
Ach ag osnaoil agus ag géarghol 's a' síor-dhéanamh bróin.

Gairim-se do gháire, do chosa 'gus do lámha,
Do dhá chích chorra bhána ós cheart-lár do chuim.
'S tú an pósaí is áille a dtug mo chroidhe grádh dhuit,
Do loit tú go bráth mé 'gus d'fhág tú mé tinn.

TRANSLATION
1. In this village dwells the fair maid, the lovely, accomplished girl. She is the brightest scion I have ever seen among women, She is my love, she is my treasure, she is the perfumed apple-blossom, She is the summer in the cold season, 'twixt Christmas and Easter. 2. 'Tis pleasant for the hen-blackbird that her mate does not beguile her, As they sit together on a single branch. Not so

22

for myself with my dearest, far from us is that condition, Groaning and weeping bitterly and ever oppressed by grief. 3. I hail your smile, your feet and your hands, Your two round white breasts over the middle of your bosom. You are the loveliest posy to whom I have given my heart, You have wounded me for ever and have left me sore.

NOTES

AIR: Noted at Deel Castle, Ballina, County Mayo in 1792 (Index p.VIII). Another copy, unarranged, in MS.29, p.122 with a similar phonetic title. [The tune is also to be found in *Crosby's Irish Musical Repository*, pp.164/165, under the title "Within this Village Dwells a Maid."]

WORDS: These verses are in Connacht Irish and their origin is probably the same as that of the tune.

There is another version, entitled "Cúilfhionn Brócach" in MS.7, No.186. I printed the words and music of a third, Eamonn Mhágáine, in the *Journal of the Irish Folk Song Society*, Vol.XX, p.51, duly annotated, with a note in Irish by my friend the late Dr. Douglas Hyde.

16. MAIDIN DOMHNAIGH
On Sunday Morning

TITLE: *1840, p.15:* Sunday Morning. Index, p.IV: Maidinn Domhnaigh.
Tune: *1840, p.15.*

WORDS: MS.10, No.59:

Maidin Domhnaigh 's mé a' dul go h-Eóchaill,
   Do casadh an óigbhean orm 's an tslighe;
Do bhí a gruaidh thrí an lasadh mar bhláth na rósa,
   Is ba bhinne liom a glór ná ceólta sidhe.
Leag mé mo láimh ar a brághaid le fóir-neart,
   Agus d'iarr mé póg uirrthi, stór mo chroidhe,
'Sé dubhairt sí, "Stad, agus ná stróic mo chlóca,
   'S ní bhfuair fios mo dhóigh-se éin-fhear ariamh."

"Níl acht sealad beag ó d'fhág mé Eóchaill,
   'S is náireach gnótha dhom tilleadh arís;
'S gur cailín falamh mé 'tá ar mearadh eóluis,
   Ar lorg a' bhóthair go Ceapach Chuinn.
Dá éis a ngeallann tú 'do bhriathraibh dhomh-sa,
   Ní ghním dod' ghlórthaibh acht suim gan bhrigh,
Do sgaoilfeadh abhaile mé gan fiú na mbróga,
   'S go bhfuair mé comhairle gan dul 'do líon!"

TRANSLATION

1. On Sunday morning as I was going to Youghal, A young girl met me on the road; She had a blushing cheek like the bloom of the rose, And her voice was sweeter to me than fairy music. I put my hand warmly round her waist, And asked her for a kiss, my heart's desire; She said, "Stop and do not tear my cloak, And I have never been familiar with any man." 2. It is only a short time since I left Youghal, And it would be a shameful business for me to go back again; I am a lively girl that has lost her way, Looking for the road to Cappoquin. After what you have promised me in your own words, I make nothing of what you say except useless talk; I would go home without even shoes, And I was advised to have nothing to do with you!"

NOTES:

AIR: No version has been found in the Bunting MSS. The tune in the *1840* volume is printed above.

The one published by my friend the late Martin Freeman in the *Journal of the Folk Song Society*, Vol VI, p.218, is one of the numerous songs (both words and music) collected by him during a prolonged stay in West Cork in 1914. Other versions go back as far as Holden's *Collection* (1806) p.14 entitled "Youghall Harbour". Bunting noted the tune in 1802 from "Redmond Stanton, at Westport".

[A tune entitled "Maidin Dia Domhnaigh" with no obvious connection with the *1840* version is to be found in MS.5, p.24. The popular ballad "Boolavogue" is a variant of Bunting's tune. In Bunting's *1796* collection there is another version printed under the title "Maidin Fhoghmhair". It is deal with in *DOSB* I, p.105 where a complete list of variants is given.]

24

WORDS: *Bunting MS.10, No.59*. "From McNally". I have not come across his name elsewhere in these MSS. Youghal is a sea-side town in the east of County Cork and Cappoquin is a few miles to the north, in County Waterford.

17. TÚ FÉIN IS MÉ FÉIN
Yourself and Myself

TITLE: *1840, p.16:* Yourself along with me. Index, p.VI: Tu fein s'me fein. Tune: MS.33, bk.4, pp.53-54.

Má thagann tú choidhche ná tar ach san oidhche,
Is siubhail go réidh 's na sgannraigh mé.
Gheobha tú an eochair faoi shál a doruis,
Is mé liom féin 's ná sgannraigh mé.

Níl pota sa' mbealach ná stól ná canna,
Ná súgán féir ná nidh fó'n ngréin.
Tá an madadh comh socair nach labhra sé focal
Ní náir dhó é — is maith mhúin mise é.

Tá mo mhaimí 'n-a codhladh 's mo dhaidí dhá bogadh,
'S a pógadh a béil, 's a' pógadh a béil
Nach aoibhinn dise 's nach truagh leat mise,
'Mo luighe liom féin ar chlumha na n-éan!

A shiúirín na gcumann stór bí aice-se,
Rún mo chléibh má b'fhíor dom féin,
'S go mb'fhearr liom bheigh id'aice ar lámh is ar leabaidh
Ná ór a' tsaoghail 's a fhagáil dom féin.

Nuair a thigim abhaile is mé lag tuirseach
I ndéigh a' lae i ndéigh a' lae,
Nuair a shínim ar mo leaba ní chorruigheann mo bhalla,
Ach mo chúl bheith léi mo chúl bheith leí.

Ní mó smut madaidh ná gnúis ar a chaile
Mun bhfaghaid sí é, mun bhfaghaid sí é
Nuair árdaigheas a stailc uirthi bíonn a' lá caite
Orm féin is í féin, mé féin is í féin.

Do bhib is do leadhb is do shean-bhríste croicinn
Do bhásaigh mé 's nár shásaigh mé,
'S gur le do chuid tuisleóga stróic tú mo phluideóga,
Tú féin is mé féin, tú féin is mé féin.

Och! is míle osna aice tá mo chroidhe tuirseach,
'S ní náir dhom é, ní náir dhom é.
Tá an oidhche ar a tosach is luaighi ar a h-obair,
Tú féin 's mé féin, tú féin 's mé féin.

TRANSLATION
1. If ever you come, don't come save at night, And walk softly and don't frighten me. You will find the key under the door, And I shall be by myself and don't frighten me. 2. There's no pot in the way, nor stool nor can, Nor a hay-rope nor anything under the sun. The dog is so quiet he won't say a word, No discredit to him — 'tis well I trained him. 3. My mammy is asleep and my daddy is fondling her, And kissing her lips, and kissing her lips, How pleasant for her, and do you not pity me Lying by myself on a feather bed? 4. Beloved sweetheart (?) My heart's desire (?) And I would rather be beside you in bed Than to have the world's gold for my own. 5. When I arrive home tired and

weary, At the end of the day, at end of day, When I lie in bed my limbs do not move, But my back is turned to her, my back is turned to her. 6. The hag's mouth is as small as a dog's, If she doesn't get it if she doesn't get it. When she gets into a temper the days is spent For myself and herself, myself and herself. 7. Your bib and your hide and your old skin breeches Were the death of me and did not satisfy me, And your restlessness tore my blankets Yourself and myself, yourself and myself. 8. Oh! she utters a thousand sighs, my heart is weary, And no shame for me no shame for me. As the night is beginning her labour lessens, Yourself and myself, yourself and myself.

NOTES

AIR: From "McDermott at Castlebar in 1802". He is probably identical with Edward MacDermott Roe, who was one of the harpers at the second Granard festival in March, 1782. Another copy (only a few notes) is found in MS.33, bk.I, p.9.

[The MS. version differs greatly from the published version and does not fit the words on account of its irregular nature. The words, however, fit the published version very well. The occasional D sharp should be read as D natural since Bunting obviously altered this note for harmonic reasons.]

WORDS: "Noted from Nancy McLoughlin, Drumin, south of Rick (Reek), 8 miles from Westport in 1802" (MS.7, No.122). As the verses are somewhat discrepant, it may be as well to explain them. The first three are addressed to a man by a girl. The fourth is his loving reply to her, but the meaning of part of the first lines is obscure. The remaining four verses refer to the woman he married.

18. RÓISÍN DUBH
The Small Black Rose

TITLE: *1840, p.16:* Black Rose Bud. Index, p.V: Roisin dubh — Black rose bud. Tune: MS.33, bk.I, p.42: "Rosheen Dubh — Little Black Rose Bud". The script is very rough and some of the notes are conjectural. It was noted from Daniel Black, harper, in 1796 (Index, VII).

WORDS: MS.7, No.59

A róisín, ná bíodh brón ort fá'r éighrigh dhuit,
Tá na bráithre 'tíocht thar sáile 'gus a' traill ar muir.
Gheobha tú párdún ón bPápa 'gus ón Róimh anoir,
Is ná spáráil fíon Spáinneach ar mo róisín dubh.

Do mharbh tú mé, a bhradóig, 's nár ba feairrde dhuit,
Is tá m'anam istigh i ngeall ort, 's ní indé ná indiu.
D'fhág tú lag marbh mé, gan sgéimh ná cruth,
'S ná déan feall orm, is tú mo leanbháinín glégheal dubh.

A róisín gheal mhómhar is áilne gnaoi,
Tá mór-ghean agam féin ort trí lár mo chroidhe.
Éaluigh liom, a chéad searc, agus fág-sa an tír,
Is má fhéadaim é déanfaidh mé báinríon díot.

'Shiubhalfainn a' drúcht leat is ciumhas na ngort,
Mar shúil go bhfuighinn súd uait is páirt de do thoil.
A chraobh álainn adubhairt liom-sa is grádh agam dhuit,
'S go ndéanfainn cleas i gcúl leasa le mo róisín dubh.

TRANSLATION

1. Little rose, do not grieve for what has happened thee, Thy kinsmen are coming across the ocean and faring over the sea. Thou wilt get pardon from the Pope and westward from Rome, And do not be sparing of Spanish wine for my small black rose. 2. You have killed me, you minx, and may it be the worse for you, My soul is pledged to you, and not yesterday nor to-day. You have left me weak and spiritless, without good looks or form, And do not deceive me, for you are my beautiful dark darling. 3. Bright little rose, gentle and fair of face, I have deep affection for you from the bottom of my heart. Elope with me, my hundred loves, and quit this land, And if I can I shall make a queen of you. 4. I would walk the dew with you and the fringe of the fields, In the hope that you would like that and would welcome it. Delightful little branch, you have told me that you love me, And I would sport behind a fairy fort with my small black rose.

NOTES

This tune and the next are variants of each other; but No.18 is a harp tune, not suitable for singing. Similarly, the Bunting MSS. have also two versions of the words, both of which can be sung to

No.19. Largely for typographical reasons. I have printed the shorter version under No.18 and the longer version under No.19. The two sets of words are from MS.7 Nos.59 and 60. They were noted respectively at Castlebar, County Mayo and at Drogheda, County Louth, the contributor and the date not being stated. As some of the references given below come from Munster, it will be seen that "Róisín Dubh" was known in all the four provinces of Ireland. In the eighteenth century, when Irish was generally spoken, it was probably the most widespread of all our folk songs.

Apart from Bunting, the following is a list of the chief printed sources, in order of date:

Hardiman's *Irish Minstrelsy* (1831), Vol.I, p.254: "Róisín Dubh" (7 verses). No tune.

The Citizen or Native Music of Ireland (1842), Nos.12 and 25: "Ros Bheag Dubh". No words. Printed from the MSS. of the great collector Henry Hudson (1798-1889), Nos. 14 and 786. The first of these two tunes was reproduced in the *Journal of the Irish Folk Song Society*, Vol.13 (1913), with a useful note on Hudson and his manuscripts.

O'Daly's *Poets and Poetry of Munster*, third edition (1851), pp.210-217: two versions and two tunes. The first (tune and poem) is entitled "Róis Gheal Dubh — Black-haired Fair Rose" and the second "Róisín Dubh — Little Black-haired Rose".

Petrie's *Ancient Music of Ireland* (1855), pp.93-95. Noted by Petrie from James Fogarty of Tibroghney, County Kilkenny. Fogarty called it "a sweet and celebrated love song" but had failed to find the words amongst the "old stock of the country". However, Petrie was able to print three verses supplied by Eugene O'Curry, the noted scholar who was a native of County Clare.

Walsh's *Irish Popular Songs*, second edition (1883), pp.60-65: "An Rós Gheal Dubh". No tune.

Joyce's *Irish Music and Song* (1888), pp.13-14: "An Róis Geal Dubh,". Tune and three verses.

Stanford's *Petrie Collection of Irish Music*, Nos.1240 and 1241. No.1240 was obtained "from Watson, County Cork" (Christian name not given). The source of 1241 is not stated. No words.

O'Curry's verses, printed by Petrie in his 1855 volume, are purely a love-song; and O'Curry assured Petrie that the versions in Hardiman and O'Daly are "corrupted by interpolations from other songs, with a view to give them a political bearing, and to convert poor *Rósín Dubh* into an allegorical personification of Ireland in the reign of Elizabeth". The basis for this incorrect statement is O'Daly's own footnote (pp. 215-217), which is as follows: "The original song of *Róisín Dubh* is supposed to have been composed in the reign of Elizabeth for the celebrated *Aodh Ua Domhnaill*, Prince of *Tír Chonaill* (Tirconnell). The allegorical allusions to Ireland under the name of *Róisín* have long been forgotten, and it is now known by the peasantry merely as a love song."

There is no reason whatever to suppose that the "original" song was composed in Elizabethan times for Red Hugh O'Donnell, who was Chief of Tirconnell, not Prince. Assisted by troops from Spain, he was one of the leaders in the war of the Irish against Elizabeth. On a visit to Spain to obtain further recruits, he died there on the 10th September, 1602 and is buried in the Franciscan Church at Valladolid. The total number of verses in the texts mentioned above is quite large, but only three have a possible "political bearing". They are: verse 1 of Bunting's No.18, which is similar to verse 2 of No.19; verse 1 of No.19; and the following *O'Daly*, p.212:

Beidh an fhairge na tuilte dearga 's an spéir na fuil,
Beidh an saoghal na chogadh chroidhearg ar dhruim na gcnoc,
Beidh gach gleann sléibhe ar fuid Eirionn 's móinte ar crith,
Lá éigin sul a n-éagfaidh mo Róis Gheal Dubh!

(The sea will be like red waves and the sky like blood,
the world will be in bloody strife on the ridge of the hills,
Every mountain valley throughout Ireland and the bogs will be
shaking,
Some day ere my Bright Black Rose will die!)

All the verse translations in O'Daly's book — about sixty in number, were done by James Clarence Mangan, a man whose poetic genius is perhaps no longer valued as it should be. In addition to his rendering of *Róisín Dubh*, he was inspired to produce his own poem *Dark Rosaleen*. It follows the original closely, and it ranks with the greatest of Anglo-Irish lyrics. I quote the first and the last of its seven verses:

O my Dark Rosaleen,
    Do not sigh, do not weep!
The priests are on the ocean green,
    They march along the deep.
There's wine from the royal Pope
    Upon the ocean green,
And Spanish ale shall give you hope,
    My Dark Rosaleen!
    My own Rosaleen!
Shall glad your heart, shall give you hope,
Shall give you health and help and hope,
    My Dark Rosaleen!

O! the Erne shall run red
    With redundance of blood,
The earth shall rock beneath our tread,
    And flames wrap hill and wood!

And gun-peal, and slogan cry
  Wake many a glen serene,
Ere you shall fade, ere you shall die,
  My Dark Rosaleen!
  My own Rosaleen!
The Judgement Hour must first be nigh,
Ere you can fade, ere you can die,
  My Dark Rosaleen!

[On p.97 of the Introduction in the *1840* Volume, Bunting gives the following note:— " 'Black Rose Bud' — a term of endearment. The melody is undoubtedly very ancient. It was sung for the Editor in 1792 by Daniel Black, the harper, who played chords in the Arpeggio style with excellent effect. The key note at the end of the strain, accompanied by the fifth and eighth, without the third, has a wailing, melancholy expression, which imparts a very peculiar effect on the melody."

Another version of the song, entitled "Mo Róis Bheag Dhubh", as collected in County Armagh in 1910 is printed in *Ceol*, Vol. 1, No. 2, p.24 by Peadar Ó Dubhda. There is no obvious connection between this version and Bunting's.]

19. RÓIS BHEAG DHUBH
The Small Black Rose

TITLE: *1840, p.17:* Second set of Black Rose Bud. Index, p.V: Roisín Bheag Dhubh — Little Black Rose Bud. Tune: *1840*, p.17.

Beidh éiclips ar na spéartha 'gus doirtfear fuil,
Tuilte tréana ó na sléibhte do strócfas cnuic,
Réabfaidh carn séadhbha is na móinteach uilig,
Nó beidh i n-aon áit sul a n-éagfaidh mo róis bheag dhubh.

A Bhriain álainn, ná bíodh cás ort fá'r éirigh dhuit,
Tá bráthair dhuit ar sáile is a' triall anoir.
Do phárdún leis ón bPápa is Róimh gan guth,
'S ná spáráil fíon Spáinneach ar do róis bheag dhubh.

Ach mharbh tú mé, a bhradóig, is féach an fearrde dhuit,
Agus m'anam féin i ngeall ort, 's ní indé ná indiu.
Mar d'fhág tú lag anbhfhann mé i gcéill 's i gcruth,
'S ná feall orm, a chaoindealbhach gheal glégheal dubh!

Bhí mé lá éigin ag siubhal le sruth,
Agus thárlaigh dham an mhaighdean is í lán don dubh,
D'fhiafraigh mé féin dí [créad]fá'r athraigh a cruth,
'S go dtiubhrainn féirín 'Bhaile an Aonaigh de bhláth na subh.

Le h-éalód fá shléibhte, fá ghleanntaibh is goirt,
Níorbh éadáil liom 'ná dhéidh sin gach a ndéanfainn ort.
Tá mo spéis is mo chéad-shearc san mbuachaill dubh,
'S le toil Dé beidh mé i ngreim leis faoi ráithe ó indiu.

A róis bheag, dár bhú liom thú dob' aoibhinn dhuit,
Cuirfinn c'laith bhuidhe 'n-a shuidhe ort ar thaobh a' chnuic.
Ná déana cleamhnas go leanbaidh i gcúl a' tuir,
Nó bhéarfaidh amhgar do *bhargain* i do shúil bheith 'gol.

Tá éan beag ar a' chraoibh-se 'tá péacach deas,
Agus éan eile i dtaoibh-se [chomh] méineamhuil leis.
'S tá éan eile sciamhach mar áirne dubh,
Agus taobh dhe chomh glégheal le bláth na subh.

Is duine buaidheartha gan chéill mé ar nós fir misc',
Is annamh fhéadaim codladh dhéanamh is táim breóite anois.
Má bhraith sí mé bheith caite claonadh, gan treóir gan mheas,
Le scaramhaint léithe ní bhfagnfar leigheas do mo scrios.

Dá bhfeicfeá mo róis sciamhach i gcúl a' tuir,
Crios San Phrainsias thart timcheall fá lár a cuirp.
Tháinic a' tám le gur shanntaigh sí an t-óigfhear glic,
Scaoil in am léithe no damnóchaidh sí an t-ord uilig.

Dar m'fhírinne, a naoidhe-bhean, dá leigfeá-sa dhamh
Culaith buidhe 'chur 'n-a shuidhe dhuit ar thaobh a' tsruth,
Bheinn seal míosa 'gcois íseal leat a' buaint na such,
Is ag imirt dísle gan sgíste le mo róis bheag dhubh.

TRANSLATION

1. There will be an eclipse in the skies and blood will be shed Strong floods from the mountains that will rend the hills, The rich(?) cairns will perish and all the bog-lands, Or . . . before my small black rose will die. 2. Handsome Brian, do not grieve for what has happened to you, One of your kinsmen is at sea, sailing from the east, Bringing your pardon from the Pope, and from Rome [without reproach] And do not spare Spanish wine for my small black rose. 3. But you have killed me, you minx, and see if you are the better for it, Though my whole soul is pledged to you — not yesterday nor to-day, For you have left me weak and forspent, in mind and body, And don't fail me, gentle and beautiful dark-haired girl! 4. One day I was walking by a stream, And I met the maiden who is so dark. I asked her why her appearance had changed, (?) [Seeing that I would give a market-town present to her whose beauty was like the raspberry blossom]. 5. With walking the mountains, the glens and the fields, I cannot think after that what I shall do [for] you. My fondness and my devotion is for [the blackhaired boy] And with God's will he shall be mine three months from to-day. 6. Little rose, if you were mine you would be happy, I would put on you a yellow dress to wear on the hill-side, Do not wed childishly behind the bush, Or the folly of your bargain will be in the tears from your eyes. 7. There is a little bird on [this] tree that is beautiful [like a] peacock, And another bird beside him [of equally friendly disposition], And another pretty bird that is like a black sloe, And one side of its body as lovely as the raspberry blossom. 8. I am a person worried and senseless, like a drunken man, It is seldom that I can sleep and now I am sick If she judged me to be forspent and deceitful, without strength of opinion By parting from her I would get no relief from my torment. 9. You should see my beautiful rose behind the bush, With the Crios of Saint Francis around her waist! The time came when she was in love with the clever young man, [Let her in time do as she pleases, or she will damn the whole order] . 9. Of a truth, my fair one, if you would allow me To put a yellow dress on you beside the stream, I would be for the space of a month secretly gathering raspberries with you. And playing dice without respite with my small black rose.

NOTES

[In the Introduction to his *1840* volume, (p.97) Bunting gives the following note:— "Little Black Rose-Bud — differs only slightly from the preceding (No.18). It is here set according to the version set in the lower Glens of the County of Antrim. The cadence at the termination seems to lean so much more to E than A that the Editor has adopted the former key-note as tonic. This curious anomaly is frequently observed in these simple airs."

There is no MS. copy of the tune and the one above is copied from the *1840* volume (p.17) with the final note changed from E to A. The tune is hexatonic with F missing and the F sharp in the key signature has therefore been omitted. Bunting's desire to end the piece on E is, no doubt, connected with his attempt to harmonise the piece in E minor.

The Index states (p.V) that the tune was noted from "a peasant of Cushendall" (Co. Antrim) in 1804.

For additional notes, see No.18, this edition.]

20. BACACH BUIDHE NA LÉIGE
The Yellow Beggar of the League

TITLE: *1840, p.18:* The Lame Yellow Beggar. Index, p.II: Bacach Buidhe na Leimneadh. Tune: MS.33, bk.3, p.8. "Boccagh Buoy Nelemnigh or The Lame Yellow Beggar".

WORDS: MS.7, No.98

Tá mo chúrsa déanta,
Saidhbhreas scaipthe ar feadh Éire,
Mo chapaill nó mo chaora,
    Ní orthu tá aon bhaoghal.
Tá mo chófraí ar gach taobh dhíom,
Is mo chuinneóg ar mo mhéaraibh,
Is mo scilling lá an aonaigh
    Le n-ól le mo mhian.

Má's bacach mé ar aon chois,
Siubhlfa' mé go h-aerach,
Is níl aon chearn do Éire
    Nach dtógfa' mé mo chíos:
Ó Chorcaigh go Dubh Éile,
'S go Baile Átha Cliath na dTéarmaí,
Go Droichead Átha na n-aontaighe
    'S go Ceannanas na Mídhe.

TRANSLATION
1. My course is finished My savings scattered all over Ireland. As to my horses or my sheep, No danger threatens them. My coffers are on each side of me, And my pail on my fingers, And my shilling on market-day To drink with my sweetheart. 2. If I am a one-legged beggar, I shall be sprightly in my walk, And there is no corner of Ireland In which I shall not collect my tribute: From Cork to Dubh Éile, And to Dublin of the [Law] Terms, To Drogheda of the fairs, And to (?) of Meath.

NOTES

TITLE: "The League" is probably the townland of that name in the parish of Myross, near Skibbereen, County Cork.

AIR: The MS. names Charles Byrne as the contributor, and the Index of *1840* names Daniel Black in 1792. Both were harpers. The printed copy (page 18) states "By O'Caghan in 1650", i.e. the celebrated Rory Dall O'Cahan. [Also, on p.91 of the Introduction to the *1840* Volume, Bunting states that it "is said to have been composed by him in reference to his own fallen fortunes, towards the end of his career".

The tune is also found in Neales *Celebrated Irish Tunes*, p.26 and Holden's *Old Established Tunes*, p.36.]

WORDS: Two versions of the song, noted from oral tradition in Munster, with nine and eleven verses, were published by me in the *Journal of the Irish Folk Song Society*, Vol.XIX (1922), pp.33-40. The two tunes printed with them differ from each other and from Bunting's.

21. AN BHRADÓG BHRÉAGACH
The pert, deceitful Minx

TITLE: *1840, p.18:* The Cunning Young Girl. Index, p.I: An bhrad-og bhreugach. Tune: MS.29, p.194.

NOTES

[The Index states that the tune was noted from Dominick O'Donnell, harper, Co. Mayo in 1810. There is a note to the same effect in MS.33, bk.5, p.20 where the tune is again to be found. In the printed version, Bunting includes D sharp for harmonic reasons.]

22. MRS. CROFTON

TITLE: *1840, p.19:* Mrs. Crofton. Index, p.II: Bain Tighearna Crofton. Tune: MS.33, bk,5, p.64: "Mrs. Crofton by Carolan in imitation of Corelli".

Is mór mo spéis san óig-mhnaoi,
Dar liom féin budh chóir sin,
Madam Crofton súgach, geanamhuil,
Bean lé'r bh'ionmhuin ceól.
'Sí do bhéaradh an leann damh
Gach oidhche, gach uair 's gach am ceart,
Leanbh deas na gcam-dhlaoi,
'Sí is uaisle ceansuidhe cáil.

TRANSLATION

Great is my regard for the young woman, Methinks that would be only right, Madam Crofton joyous and beautiful, A woman who delights in music. It is she who would give me ale Every night, every hour, on every due occasion, The pretty lass with the curly locks, Most noble in her gentle nature.

NOTES

AIR: Noted from Charles Fanning in 1792.

WORDS: Connellan's *An Duanaire (Fonna Seanma)*, 1829, p.5. Both words and air are by Carolan and are printed in my edition (1958): the air in Vol.I, p.178 and the words in Vol.II, pp.18-19. The words run to 28 lines, but as they are wholly of an adulatory character I have thought it sufficient to print the first eight, with a translation.

The Croftons came to Ireland in Elizabethan times, and their history is given in the *Crofton Memoirs* by Henry Thomas Crofton (1911). The subject of the present piece is Elizabeth, wife of James Crofton of Longford House, on the northerly slope of the Ox Mountains, a few miles west of Ballysodare, County Sligo. This family was Catholic and James Crofton became the owner of the family property in circumstances recounted in the *Memoirs*:

"Edward Crofton, who was a Justice of the Peace for Sligo, had a large family, fifteen in all. He had married in 1680, and about 1729 James, his third son, fell violently in love with Elizabeth, daughter of Captain Edward Robinson, of Sligo. She was a Protestant, and the father of each was bitterly opposed to the match. James tried in vain to win his father's consent. At last, acting on the principle that 'all is fair in love and war', he decided to become a Protestant. His father threatened to cut him off with a shilling if he did so, and he retorted that two could play at that game, and he would turn informer and claim a forfeiture of the family estates unless his father would consent the marriage, but the unhappy Edward absolutely declined to make any terms with his son.

The end was that the Book of Converts at Dublin records that on February 18, 1731-2, James's sister Ursula "conformed", and two days later "James Crofton, gent." did so.

James followed this up by filing a Bill in Chancery against his father, stating that he had been a Papist like his father and eldest brother, but his eyes were now open to the errors of the Roman Church, and he claimed delivery of a deed relating to the property, which he alleged was witheld from him in order to deprive him of his rights.

His father replied that he and his eldest son remained firm to their faith, and that James had often threatened to leave his Church in order to gain the reward offered to those who denounced Papist recusants, and for this reason he had changed his faith and denounced his father and brother."

James obtained the family estates and duly married Elizabeth Robinson. His two elder brothers, having forfeited their property as a result of his apostasy, left Ireland for France, where one of them subsequently became an Archbishop and the other Governor of La Hogue.

23. JACK THE JOLLY PLOUGHBOY

TITLE: *1840, p.20:* The jolly ploughman. Index, p.II: An toireamh sugach.
Tune and words: MS.33, bk.5, p.22.

'Twas Jack the jolly ploughboy
  Was ploughing in his land,
Cried "yough" unto his horses
  And boldly bid them stand.
Then Jack sat down upon his plough
  And thus began to sing,
And Jack he sung his song so sweet
  He made the valleys ring

Chorus:
With his toorannan nanty na,
Sing toorannan nanty na,
Sing toorannan toorannan toorannan, toorannan,
Toorannan nanty na.

NOTES
Bunting prints the words under the notes of the music. "From J. Duncan, Harper, 1792" (Index p.XI).

The tune was used by Samuel Lover for his best-known song, 'The Low-Back'd Car'.

Alfred Moffat prints the song in his *Minstrelsy of Ireland*, pp.12-13. It has four verses, to Bunting's tune. The first verse and the chorus are Bunting's, somewhat altered; the authorship of the other three verses is unstated, but presumably they were written by Moffat himself.

The earliest version of the air appears to be in Aird's *Scotch English, Irish and Foreign Affairs*, Vol.III (1788), p.160, with the title "To Rodney we will go". Moore used another version for his beautiful song "Farewell — but whenever you welcome the hour" in the Fifth Number of his *Irish Melodies* (1813), No.9, giving the name of the tune as "Moll Roone". I have not found this title, and Moore's source appears to be the tune called "The Drop of Dram" in O'Farrell's *Pocket Companion*, bk.IV.

[Different words and music are also to be found in Stanford's *Songs of Old Ireland*, p.54. In *Folk Songs of the West Country*, collected by Baring-Gould, the song entitled 'A Hunting we will go' (p.12) is a variant of Bunting's tune. Another version is to be found in *Six Suffolk Folk Songs*, by E.J. Moeran, entitled 'Nutting Song'.]

24. SLIABH GAILLEAN
Slieve Gallen

TITLE: *1840, p.21* Slieve Gallen. Index, p.VI Sliabh Guillean. Tune: MS.33, bk.3, p.32. "From Hugh Higgins, died in 1796. Very ancient."

NOTES

Bunting states (Introduction, p.96) that this is "a Ballinascreen air, arranged by Lyons in 1700". Ballinascreen is in County Derry, and Slieve Gallen is a mountain in the same county.

[The Index p.X states that the piece was collected from "Higgins, harper, County Roscommon".

Hardebeck prints a song in *Seoda Ceoil*, Part I, p.3, called "Slieve Gallen Braes" but there is no connection between the two tunes. The words which begin "As I went a walking one morning in May", do not fit the Bunting tune. There is another copy of the tune in MS.33, bk.5, p.77.]

25. IS MAITH LE NÓRA CÍSTE
Nora Likes Cake

TITLE: *1840, p.V:* Onóra an chisde — Nora with the cake. But the title in the English index (p.IX) is "Nora with the purse" and this is repeated over the tune (p.22). The difference is explained by the similarity of the two Irish words: "císte" means "cake", and "ciste" (without the accent) means "purse".

TUNE: MS.33, bk.2, p.21

An bóthar ó thuaidh, an bóthar ó thuaidh,
An bóthar ó thuaidh go Tráighlí,
An bóthar ó thuaidh 's an cómhngar a dtuaidh,
's an bóthar ó thuaidh go Tráighlí.

Is maith le Nóra prátaí rósta,
Is maith le Nóra císte,
Is maith le Nóra ana-chuid feóla,
Agus bainne na ngabhar san oidhche.

Do ghearra-chos deas, do ghearra chos deas,
Do ghearra chos deas a Nóra,
Do ghearr-chos deas ó'n ghlún go dtí an t-alt,
Is tá an leanbh ar fad go córach.

Corruigh do chos is corruigh do chos
Is chorruigh do chos, a Sheáinín,
Corruigh do chos, do chroidhe is do chorp.
Is beimíd go luath i dTráighlí.

TRANSLATION

1. The road from the north, the road from the north, The road from the north to Tralee, The road from the north and the neighbourhood to the north And the road from the north to Tralee. 2. Nora likes roast potatoes, Nora likes cake, Nora likes lots of meat, And the goats milk at night. 3. Your lovely small limbs, your lovely small limbs, Your lovely small limbs, Nora Your lovely small limbs, from knee to ankle, And the girl is altogether charming. 4. Stir your feet and stir your feet, And stir your feet, Johnny, Stir your feet your heart and your body, And we shall soon be in Tralee.

NOTES

AIR: Noted from Byrne the harper in 1802. [A variant of this tune (which is in single jig rhythm) called 'The Maid of the Spinning Wheel', is still played today as a four part double jig. A full list of variants is given in the notes to tune No.1 in Breathnach's *Ceol Rince na hÉireann*.]

WORDS: I have copied these from the booklet *Cosa Buidhe Arda*, pp.23/4. This collection, with the tunes in tonic solfa was noted from oral transmission by my friend the late Fionán MacColuim of County Kerry, whose native language was Irish. It consists of about forty songs, intended for children.

My first verse of our song is used as a chorus for the remaining verses. I have made minor changes. MacColuim gives as the second line of verse 2, "Is maith le Nóra an t-im leo", meaning "Nora likes butter with them", i.e. with roast potatoes. Our MS. has "císte" instead of "an t-im leo". Neither the assonance nor the metre is affected. The second half of the tune is most suitable for the chorus.

41

26. BRUACH NA CARRAIGE BÁINE
The Edge of the White Rock

TITLE: *1840, p.22:* The brink of the white rocks. Index, p.II: Bruachna carraige baine. Tune: MS.33, bk.3, p.48 — "From Hugh Higgins' singing".

B'fhearr liom féin ná Éire mhór,
    Nó saidhbhreas Rígh na Spáinne,
Nó a bhfeice mé do ór buidhe le mo ló,
    Go mbeinn-se ag ól do shláinte:
Tusa 'gus mise bheith pósta, a ghrá,
    Le lán-toil t-athar is máthar,
A mhaighdean óg is milse póg
    Le taobh na carraige báine.

A chiúin-bhean óg na ngruadh mar rós,
    Is truagh gan mise leat pósta,
Gan ghruaim, gan bhrón ó nidh ar a' domhan,
    Acht siubhal go suidheamhail i gcóiste.
Rún gach duine 'sí an stáid-bhean,
    A cúl trom dualach fáinneach,
An ríoghan óg is milse póg
    Le taobh na carraige báine.

TRANSLATION
1. I would rather than all Ireland, Or the riches of the King of Spain, Or all I shall ever see in my life of yellow gold, That I would be drinking your health: You and I to be married, my love, With the full consent of your father and mother, Young maiden of the sweetest kisses Beside the white rock. 2. O gentle young woman with cheeks like the rose, 'Tis a pity that I am not wedded to you, Without gloom or sadness from anything in the world, But moving sedately

in a carriage. Beloved by all is the beautiful woman, With her heavy, plaited, ringletted tresses, The young queen of the sweetest kisses Beside the white rock.

NOTES

AIR: Noted from a blind man at Westport in 1802 (Index, p.X). It exists in a number of versions, five of which are printed in Petrie's *1855 volume*, pp.137 to 143, with valuable notes. There are inferior copies in MS.29, pp.187 and 196, and in MS.33, bk.5, p.38 (used for the *1840* volume). In MS.33, bk.4, p.20 there is a different version.

WORDS: From MS.7, No.78, the name of the contributer not being stated. Other versions have been published, notably one of eight stanzas in O'Daly's *Poets and Poetry of Munster*, third edition, (1851), pp.280-285; but the translation and notes are completely unreliable.

27. AN DOCHÚIR SEÁN Ó HAIRT
Dr. John Hart

TITLE: *1840, p.III:* Cupán Ní Ara — Doctor John Hart. The Irish title is incorrectly spelt and belongs to a different song, Cupán Uí Eaghra (O'Hara's Cup), composed by Carolan for Kean O'Hara of Nymph'sfield, County Sligo (my edition of Carolan, I, pp.233/4 and II, pp.80/81). Tune: MS.33, bk.1, pp.36/37: "Dr. John Hart by Signor Carollini".

Bhéara mé anois an chuairt seo gan bhréig,
Mar a bhfuil an sagart geanamhail d'uaslibh árd Gaodhal,
Fear breágh íoghmhar tapaidh,
Fear a riarfadh gasruidhe,
Ar Sheán Ó hAirt go ceart a labhraimse féin:
Fear den aicme scapfadh fíon go réidh,
Is d'ólfadh go fras le mac a' cheóil is a' léigheann.
Da mbéinn san Róimh mar b'ait liom
Is bíodh mo roghain ionghlachtha,
Is cinnte go ndéanfainn easbog mór dhíot féin.

Leigheas do phreab ar aicíd glórthaí a bhéil,
Go mba buan é i bhfad is clú do'n ór é go léir:
Níl fear, níl bean ná leanbh
Bheigh ar easbuidhe teagaisg

Nach ndéanfadh seisean seanmóir mhór dhóibh le céill.
Stíobhard ceart do Mhac na glóire é féin,
Préalóid beannuighthe de mhór-fhol Uí Néill.
Níl sin uair na tráth
Dá bhfuighinn-se uain ar chách
Nach n-ólfainn suas gan spás do shláinte breágh féin!

TRANSLATION

1. I shall now certainly pay this visit To the kindly priest of the great Irish nobility, A fine, clever, enthusiastic man, A man who could command multitudes, It is of John Hart that I speak thus properly: A man of the type that readily dispenses wine, And would drink freely with musicians and scholars. If I were in Rome as I should like to be, And if my choice were acceptable, Be sure that I would make an archbishjop of you! 2. A speedy cure for illness is the sound of his voice, Long life to him, he is renowned of all the clergy: There is no man, woman or child Who is in need of instruction To whom he will not give a great and wise sermon. He is a righteous servant of the Son of glory

A blessed prelate of the great blood of O'Neill There is no time or occasion,
If I got the opportunity from everybody That I would not straightaway drink
your own good health!

NOTES

AIR: The Index of *1840* states that the air was noted from Hugh
Higgins, the harper, in 1792. Bunting's rough notation is in MS.
29, p.86, from which he seems to have produced the fair copy in
MS.33, bk.3, pp.36/7. This is provided with a bass in MS.33, bk.5,
p.44, whence the tune is printed in the *1840* volume. There is
an inferior version in MS.33, bk.4, p.47. [With the tune as printed
above from MS.33, bk.3, pp.36/7, there is also a bass, similar to
that in the *1840* piece.]

WORDS: From Connellan's *Dunaire (Fonna Seanma)*, 1829, p.2.
Both words and air are by Carolan and are printed in my edition of
his work (Vol. I, p.192 and Vol. II, pp.33/4).

According to W. Maziere Brady's *Episcopal Succession*, Vol.II,
p.191, Dr. John Hart succeeded to the See of Achonry by Brief
dated the 30th September, 1735. As his successor was appointed
in August, 1739, he presumably died before that date; but he was
living in the previous April, as a vellum pedigree of the MacDermots
of Coolavin bears his holograph signature under 8th April, 1739:
"Johannes O'Hart, Ep.Ac" (Bishop of Achonry).

Some details regarding the bishop are given in Archdeacon
O'Rorke's *History of the Parish of Ballsadare and Kilvarnet* (1878),
p.198 *et seq.* Under the Penal Laws, no Catholic could possess a
legal title to land, and it was customary for Catholic landowners
to transfer the legal title to a Protestant friend, who thereafter
held the property in trust − a trust that was very rarely abused.
Dr. John Hart and his brother Charles were the owners of Cloonmahon, County Sligo; and, following the usual practice, they made
the estate over to a Protestant neighbour named Betteridge. He,
however, repudiated the trust and took the property to his own
use − and abuse for which the law, of course, provided no remedy.
Thereupon, another Protestant neighbour, O'Hara of Annaghbeg,
took Dr. John Hart to live with him and, in O'Rorke's words, "did
all that courtesy and kindness could do to make up for the loss of
Cloonmahon".

The bishop was renowned for his hospitality, and O'Rorke mentions his kindness to birds, particularly caged birds, which he re-
leased wherever possible. There is a pleasing legend that when he
died all the birds of the locality assembled at his funeral and chanted
his requiem. In the second verse of the song, Carolan speaks of his
religious zeal for every man, woman and child, calls him "a righteous servant of the Son of glory", and alludes to the fact that on his
mother's side he was of the princely blood of O'Neill.

The distinguished writer Charles O'Conor of Belnagare, who was a contemporary of Dr. Hart and knew him well, says that this song "has often excited sentiments of the most fervent piety" (Walker's *Irish Bards*, p.316). He adds: "It is a loss to the public that this truly virtuous dignitary had been so insensible to all emotions of self-love as to have the first of Carolan's compositions for him entirely suppressed." It is evident from the context that O'Conor is referring to the present song, for he quotes a line of it; so that the attempt to suppress it was not successful. O'Conor seems to imply that Carolan composed more than one song for Dr. Hart, but no other song has been found.

28. NÓIRÍN MO MHÍLE STÓIRÍN
Nóirín my thousand treasures

TITLE: *1840, p.24:* Nora My Thousand Treasures. Index, p.V: Nóirín mo mhíle stóirín. Tune: MS.33, bk.4, p.48 — "A Nóra, a mhíle Stórach".

NOTES
[The Index p.IX states that it was noted "at Galway. 1802". The tune is also found in MS.5, p.68 with the title "Noreen Ma Villa Storeen". This is the version used by Bunting for publication. There appears to be a bar missing at the end of the first section of the MS. version printed above. Reading from bar 5 the phrase might be reconstructed as follows:]

29. CISTE NÓ STÓR
Treasures or Wealth

TITLE: *1840, p.24, No.29:* "My Love and Treasure". Index: p.III: Ciste sa Stór. Tune: MS.33, bk.2, p.71: "Collected in 1802 in Connaught".

WORDS: MS.7, No.38

Ciste nó stór go deóigh ní mholfad,
Acht imirt is ól is céol do ghnáth.
Taoim ar baois fá mhnaoi 's ní ró-mhaith a chodlaim,
'S nach truagh sin duine ar bith beó mar táim!

'Sé fáth mo thuirse nach bhfaghaim do chuideacht,
A mhaighdean tséimh, mas gnaoi leat mé,
Suidh go dlúth le mo thaobh is tabhair póg dom' bhéal,
Agus cuingidh dhuit féin ón mbás mé.

Is truagh gan mise 'gus an óig-bhean tséimh
In uaigneas coille fá bharraibh na gcraobh,
Go n-imireamois cluiche beag soilbhir séimh,
Le súgradh is éigne grádhmhar.

A chara na gcumann, nach súgach a bhéinn
'S mé a' síor-thabhairt aire le ceól na n-éan,
Mo rún a bheith agam 's mé a' pógadh a béal,
Is ag imirt ar poinnte grádh léi!.

TRANSLATION
1. Treasure or wealth I ne'er would esteem, But gambling and drink and music all the time. I'm mad about a woman and I don't sleep very well, And isn't it a pity for any living being to be as I am! 2. The cause of my affliction is the lack of your company. O lovely maid, if I am to your liking, Sit close to my side and give my lips a kiss, And join me to yourself and save me from death. 3. It is a pity that the gracious young woman and I, Are not in the loneliness of a wood beneath the trees, Playing a little gentle happy game, With fun and loving wisdom. 4. Dearest love, how happy would I be To listen for ever to the music of the birds, My sweetheart beside me and I kissing her mouth, And playing at the point of love with her!

NOTES
AIR: Printed in the Introduction to *1840*, p.13 with the title "Ciste no Stor — Coffers nor stores". It is repeated in a more elaborate form on p.24 of the same volume with the wrong title "My Love and

47

Treasure". The difference between the two versions illustrates the unreliability of the tunes printed in Bunting's last volume. According to the Index of *1840*, this melody (and probably the appropriate words) were "From Dr. Young, Bishop of Clonfert at Castlereagh, County Roscommon, in 1800". [Bunting notes (in p.96 of the preface, *1840* volume) that this tune "seems to have been the original of Carolan's 'Fairy Queen' the only difference being that Carolan added two parts to it, in which it was generally played by the harpers". 'The Fairy Queen' is dealt with extensively in *DOSC* Vol.II, p.116-17 and also in Willis' edition of *Neales Celebrated Irish Tunes*, No.17.

Versions of the tune occur in Holden (1806/7) Vol.II, p.3, "O! Save me from Death"; Holden (post 1806) Vol.I, p.5, "Save me from Death"; and in Mulholland (1810) p.56, "Hide me from Death". The origin of these titles may be found in the final line of the second stanza, above.]

WORDS: MS.7, No.38. I have seen no other version of the words.

30. BUALADH TRIAILL CHUM TSEÓIL
Getting ready to sail

TITLE: *1840, p.25:* Preparing to sail way. Index, p.II: Buileam tréal chum tseoil. Tune: MS.33, bk.2, p.23 — "Borlin treal an shuile — or Preparing to sail away. One of Joyce Country tunes. Got in Ballinrobe". Many of the note values are uncertain.

There is also a rough unbarred copy in MS.29, p.135. The Index, p.IX states that the tune was collected "at Ballinrobe in 1792". [Notice the unusual, though very effective, use of five bar phrases in the MS. version above. Bunting in the *1840* volume, took from the tune by extending the cadential points to make more conventinal two-bar phrases.]

31. CAILÍN NA GRÚAIGE DUIBHE
The Black-haired Girl

TITLE: *1840, p.25:* The Black-haired Girl. Index, p.II: Cailin na gruaige duibhe. Tune: *1840*, p.25, No.31.

NOTES

According to Bunting's Index, he obtained this air from George Petrie in 1822. It would appear to be an instrumental setting of a song air but I have found no words with this title either in Bunting's MSS. or elsewhere.

32. SÉAMAS ÓG PLUINCÉAD
Young James Plunkett

TITLE: *1840, p.26:* Young James Plunket. Index, p.V: Seamus og. Tune: MS.33, bk.2, p.31: "Grạdh na mban og or James Plunket. From Charles Byrne".

Séamas Óg Pluinceád, bronntóir an fhíona,
Fuair oideas ar cheóltaibh, spóirt agus aoibhneas,
Ar Laidin, ar Ghréigis 's ar Ghaoidhlig bhréagh líomtha,
Grádh na mban óg é, an t-óigfhear glan saoitheamhail.

Is fearr ná sin féin a mhéinn is a mhaitheas,
Guaire níor thug buadh air i n-uaisleacht a bhearta.
Go mba fada saoghlach beó é, gan bhrón ar bith ná easbaidh,
'N-a árd-fhlaith mhór bhéarfadh ól fada do ghasraidh.

An gcualaidh sibh tréithe an tréan-mharcaigh shúgaigh,
Mar atá Pluincéadach glégeal bréagh, éadtrom lúthmhar?
'Sé dubhairt gach maighdean bhéasach 'mbíodh na céadta dhi ag umhlú,
Mo léan! gan mé is tú mar aon ar ár nglúinibh!

Níl aon maighdean bhéasach ó Éirne go Gaillimh amach,
Dá gcualadh riamh a thréithe ná'r mhéinn leó bheith i n-aice seal.
I gcoilltibh Bhuin an Fhiodáin tá an furránach breágh soineanta,
Mheallfadh na cailíní ar chúl na geraoibheaca.

TRANSLATION
1. Young James Plunkett, bestower of wine, Reared in melody, sport and pleasure, In Latin, in Greek and in fine polished Irish, He is the beloved of

young women, the bright, well-bred young man. 2. Better than that are his disposition and his kindliness, Guaire never exceeded him in nobility of behaviour, Long may he live, without the slightest sorrow or need, As a great chieftain giving abundant cheer to his followers. 3. Have you heard of the traits of this fine joyous knight, Plunket the handsome, the fine, light and nimble. Says every fair maiden whom hundreds are courting Alas! that you and I are not united on our knees! 4. Not a single maiden from the Erne down to Galway Who has not heard of his good qualities and longs for his company. In the woods of Bunenedin dwells this fine hearty young man, Who would court the girls in the shade of the branches.

NOTES

AIR: Three versions occur in Bunting's MSS. One, Ms.33, bk.5, p.21, was noted from James Duncan and was used for printing in *1840*. The second, greatly superior, was noted from Charles Byrne and is printed above. [The third is a rough notation in Ms.29, p. 195]. I have found no other version in any book or manuscript. Though Bunting does not attribute it to Carolan, it is possible that he composed it, since he is undoubtedly the author of the appropriate words (see *DOSC* I, p.243 and II, p.96).

[The tune of the Connemara song "Moll Dubh a' Ghleanna" is a variant of Bunting's tune.]

WORDS: None in these manuscripts. I have chosen the copy in "Hardiman" (1831) p.82, which is the only one that gives the last verse. Not much is known about the subject of our song. Hardiman states (p.129) that he was James Plunkett of Bunenedin, County Sligo, but it is probable that he merely derived this information from the fourth verse. In one of the manuscript versions, "Bun an fhiodáin" is corrected to "Cill an fhiodán" with a scribal note, "The seat of Mr. Plunket, near Mr. Brown's of Cloonfad in the parish of Aughrim, Co. Roscommon." Another manuscript has the following note in pencil: "James Plunkett of Kilanadin near Elphin died at Patt. McGarry's in the greatest distress."

Cloonfad townland, house and Lough are in the County Roscommon, on the Leitrim border and about four miles south of Jamestown. Further south again is Castle Plunkett, which was presumably the seat of another branch of this celebrated Roscommon family.

Guaire, mentioned in the second verse, was a famous King of Connacht in the sixth century. Some anecdotes about him, derived from the ancient manuscripts are given in Dr. Douglas Hyde's *Literary History of Ireland* (1900), pp.168 and 395/8.

33. SIR CHARLES COOTE

TITLE: *1840, p.26:* Planxty Charles Coote. Index, p.V. Plancstae Sealuis Cuta.
Tune: Ms.33, bk.3, p.50. "Charles Coote by Carolan. Plangsty. From Rose
Mooney".

NOTES

As in the case of the previous air, the sole source is Bunting, who
noted it from Rose Mooney in 1800. It is by Carolan, who presumably composed words for it; but these have not been found
(see *DOSC* Vol.1 No.33 and Vol.2, p.14). [There is a rough second
copy of the tune in MS.29, p.200.]

The first settler in Ireland of the Coote family was Sir Charles
Coote, 1st Baronet (cr. 2nd April, 1621), whose successors claim the
title of Premier Baronet of Ireland. He served in the wars against
O'Neill, Earl of Tyrone, at the head, as Captain, of 100 foot, with
which he was present at the siege of Kinsale in 1601. During the
rebellion of 1641-2 he was "at one time forty-eight hours on horseback when, in April, 1642, effecting the famous passage through
Mountrath woods for the relief of Birr". Of the host of murderous
marauders who infested Ireland at this period he was probably the
worst. He it was, for example, who excused the butchery of young
children in Wicklow on the grounds that "nits will become lice".
His seat was at Castle Cuffe, Queen's County, and he was M.P. for
the county from 1639 to 1642, when he was "slain by the rebels".
To commemorate the Mountrath exploit, his heir, who was a true
son of his father, was created Earl of Mountrath, 6th September,
1660.

The subject of Carolan's air may be either the 4th Baronet or the 5th Baronet, both of whom were named Charles. The former was born c.1635, succeeded to the title 30th August, 1672, married Isabella, daughter of the Earl of Carnarvon in 1675, and died 29th May, 1709. He was succeeded by his son, who was born c.1680 and died at Bordeaux on the 14th September, 1715. In Carolan's time, the family seat was Coote Hall, on the river Shannon a few miles east of Boyle, County Roscommon. But its fortunes were declining, and Maurice O'Connor, head of one of the most powerful Catholic families in Tudor days, had become enormously wealthy. Practically penniless, because his patrimony had been escheated by the Crown, he had left for London about 1700 and became nominally a Protestant in order to become a member of the Inner Temple. As such, he became one of the great leaders of the Bar. Part of his enormous wealth was invested in real estate, and by 1720 he owned practically the whole of Tunbridge Wells. But the call of his native land seems to have been insistent, and shortly afterwards he sold the whole of his English estates and returned to Ireland. He married Lady Mary Plunkett, daughter of the Earl of Fingall, who was head of one of the most distinguished Catholic families; and he bought Coote Hall from the Coote family for £7500 — a very large sum in those days.

Carolan composed three tunes for Maurice O'Connor and one for his wife (my edition, Vol. 1 Nos. 115-118 and Vol.II, pp.72-75). This is No.115, with the words of three quatrains, of which the first is:

Is iongantach an chúis é 's is nuaidheacht sa' tír,
Ó Conchubhair a' ceannach dúithche 's a' Cútach dhá dhíol.

Má leantar don chúrsa so a réir mar cuireadh tús air,
Beidh Gaedhealuibh go súgach sa' gcúigeadh so arís.

(This is a wonderful affair and a novelty in the country,
O'Connor buying an estate and Coote selling it.
If this process continues as it has begun,
The Irish will be joyful in this province again.'

In the remaining verses, Carolan gives thanks to God and welcomes "Young O'Connor Faly" from London to Ireland.

34. SÚSAÍ NÍ CHEALLAIGH
Susanna Kelly

TITLE: *1840, p.27:* Saely Kelly. Index, p.V: Sheela ni Kelly. Tune: MS.33, bk.3, p.16, 17.

NOTES

Bunting obtained this tune from Patrick Linden at Newtown Hamilton, County Armagh in 1802, according to the Index of *1840*. But the MS. copy from which he printed it states that he noted it from Charles Byrne. In a note over the tune he has: "By Thomas Connallon about 1660", whereas it was composed by Carolan, born ten years later. Finally, he gives the Christian name as Sheela and Saely (?Sally), whereas the girl's name was Susanna.

The name Kelly is, with the exception of Murphy, the most common surname in Ireland, and their principal habitat in Carolan's time was the County Roscommon. Skeffington Gibbon, who was a Roscommon man, says in his *Memoirs* (1829, p.23): "I asked my father which were the most ancient and respectable Kellys. His answer was that the head of the Protestant aristocracy of that name were those of Castle Kelly, Cargins, Kiltoom, Mucklin and Churchborough; the Catholics are those of Tycoole, Turrock, Scregg and Ballymurray. As for the barony of Athlone, says he, I wish to leave it as God left the Jews". Edmond Kelly, son of John Kelly of Scregg, settled at Churchborough, in the barony of Athlone, and Susanna Kelly was probably his daughter. This is indicated by the first verse of the words, quoted below. The song consists of three stanzas in Carolan's usual style, two of which are printed in Ó Máille's edition of the poet, p.151. Bunting has all three, noted by Patrick Lynch from "John MacDermud", a shoemaker of Castlebar, on the 27th May, 1802.

Is i mbarúnta Bhaile Átha Luain
    Tá'n chiúin-bhean bhreágh do bhaor mé,
Súsaí shéimh Ní Cheallaigh,
    Plúr na mban Gaodhlach.
Is righin-réidh a rosg, is ró-bhreágh a folt,
    Agus is seang, singil a cúm gléigeal;
Ní bréag ná stair adubhras leat,
    A Shúsaí dheas na bpéarlaí.

(In the barony of Athlone/Is the gentle fair lady that has troubled me,/Gentle Susie Kelly,/Flower of the Irish women./Steady and clear are her eyes, beautiful her tresses,/Graceful and slender her lovely form; What I have told you is neither flattering nor false,/Handsome Susie of the pearly teeth.)

[The words are in Ms.18,p.62 with a fair copy in Ms.7, No.71. There are four other notations of the tune in the Bunting MSS:
    MS.29, p.24: "Miss Sally Kelly"
    MS.29, p.25: "Plangsty Ward. Miss Sally Kelly"
    MS.33, bk.4, p.12 — in common time: "Celia sul-ghlas ini Cheallaighe"
    MS.33, bk.5, (p.83): "Miss Sally Kelly": the copy used for the 1840 Volume.
The version of the tune printed above had only one sharp in the MS. with the C sharp written in throughout.
See also DOSC I No.75 and II pp.47-48.]

35. AN DEILADÓIR
The Wheelwright

TITLE: *1840, p.28:* An deladóir — The wheelwright. Index, p.I: An deileadóir.
Tune: MS.33, bk.I, p.7: "An dealadoir. The wheelwright." No time or key signature.

WORDS: MS. 7, No. 84

Mallacht Rígh na hAoine
    ar a' maol-chnoc so 'bhfuilim ann,
Gur fuide lá go n-oidhch' ann
    ná bliadhain ar a' mbaile úd thall.
Is ann nach gcuirthí iongnamh
    dá ndéanamois súgradh is greann,
Ach na coirníní buidhe dhá líonadh,
    's iad a bheith lán den lionn.

Rachainn féin don Gréig leat,
    a théagair is a mhíle stór,
Agus thillinn ar m'ais arís leat
    ag éisteacht le fuaim do ghlóir.
Ba bheag liom-sa mar féirín duit-se
    a chéad is dhá mhíle bó;
A phlúir 's a sgoith an aonaigh,
    ná tréig choidhche an deiladóir!

Tá mé ins an áit seo
    Ó Fheil' Pádraic gan deór den lionn,
Is cinnte dá bhfaghainn bás
    gurab' é m'árus an chill úd thall.

Dá dtóigheadh Righ na ngrása
    an ceó so 'tá ós mo chionn,
Go n-ólfainn-se féin sláinte
    chúil álainn mo chailín duinn.

TRANSLATION

1. The curse of (Good) Friday's King on this bare hill on which I am, A day and night on it is longer than a year in yonder townland . 'Tis there would be no cause for wonder if we made fun and frolic, But the tawny tankards flowing, and they full of ale. 2. I would myself fare to Greece with you, my darling and my thousand treasures, And I would come back again with you, listening to the sound of your voice. I would reck little as a gift for you one hundred and two thousand kine; O flower and blossom of the market-place, do not ever forsake the wheelright! 3. I am in this spot Since Saint Patrick's Day without a drop of ale; 'Tis certain that if I should die my habitation would be yonder churchyard. If the King of graces were to lift the trouble that is over me, I myself would drink health to the lovely tresses of my brown-haired girl.

NOTES

AIR: I have not come across any version of Bunting's air or words either printed or manuscript. [The Index (p.XI) gives the source as "P. Lynch, Castlebar, 1803." The date should read '1802' to coincide with Bunting's visit to Mayo in that year. There is another copy of the tune in MS.33, bk.5, p.36 and this was the one used by Bunting for printing.

Bríd Granville of Dunquin, Co. Kerry, sings a song entitled "Beannacht Ó Rí na hAoine", the words of which are related to those printed above. The tune, however, is not related. In the *1840* version, Bunting repeated the first phrase, thus putting the tune out of synchronisation with the words. Thomas Davis, however, wrote his song "The Penal Days" to the air as printed in the *1840* volume.]

WORDS: MS.7, No.84. Noted in 1802 from "John MacDermud, Shoemaker, Castlebar."

36. MAGUIRE'S LAMENTATION

TITLE: *1840, p.28:* Maguire's Lamentation. Index, p.III: Cuma Mic Guidhir. Tune: 1840, p.28, No.36.

NOTES

There is no MS. copy. "Noted from C. Martin, Harper, Virginia, County Cavan" [Index p.IX].

In the absence of words, it cannot be said for whom this elegy was composed. Maguire is the name of a great family of Fermanagh, formerly one of the most powerful in Ulster. They were chiefs of the county for centuries until the confiscation of Ulster in the reign of James I.

37. BÓ MAOL
The Hornless Cow

TITLE: *1840, p.29:* Bó Maol — The Hornless Cow. Index, p.II: Bó Mhaol. Tune: MS.5, p.39: "The hornless cow". No key or time signature, but with some accidentals written in.

NOTES

[The Index (p.X) states that the piece was collected from "T. Conlan, 1833". A comparison of the MS. with two printed versions shows how Bunting not only changed the implied time signature but also discarded the 'flattened 7th' in order to fit the tune into the Ionian Mode (or Major scale). Tune No. 686 in O'Neill's *Dance Music of Ireland* is a reel called 'The Hornless Cow'. There is no obvious connection between it and the Bunting tune apart from a similar time signature.]

38. SÍN SÍOS AGUS SUAS LIOM
Lie up with me and lie down with me

TITLE: *1840, p.30:* Down beside me. Index, p.V: Sín sios agus suas liom.
Tune: MS.33, bk.2, p.12.

NOTES

The manuscript gives the source of the tune as follows: "from Denis a Hempson, Hugh Higgins and Mrs. Bristow, who was taught it by Dominic Mungan."

[The Index (p.X) states that it was noted from "D. Black, Harper in 1796". In the introduction to the *1840* volume, Bunting says that the piece was "taken from the performance of Dominic Mungan, the celebrated harper the father of Bishop Warburton".

Similar versions of the tune are in the following printed collections:

59

Wright's *Aria di Camera* (c.1730) p.40
Neale's *Celebrated Irish Tunes* (c.1726) p.17
Thompson's *Hibernian Muse* (c.1786) p. 59
Holden's *Collection of Old-Established Irish Slow and Quick tunes* (1806/7) bk. 2, p.18
Holden's *Collection of Most Esteemed Old Irish Melodies* bk.I, p.48 (post 1806)

In *Ceol*, Vol.V, No.1 pp.2/3, Breandáin Breathnach reproduces a music sheet from the British Library entitled "An Irish song sung by Mr. Abell at his consort at Stationers Hall". A phonetic form of the Irish words appears set to the tune in the original sheet which is undated but has been assigned to 1714. Breathnach points out that it is probably the first Irish air with associated words to have appeared in print, and he links it with another version of the air entitled "The Banks of Banna".]

39. KITTY O'HARA

TITLE: *1840, p.30:* Kitty O'Hara. Index, p.III: Caitlín Ní Aghra. Tune: MS.33, bk.2, p.77: "Cata Ni Ara". Origin not stated.

NOTES

[The Index (p.IX) states that the piece was collected "at Castlebar, 1802". In the *1840* version, Bunting repeats the second section, and includes a flattened seventh not present in the MS. version.]

40. TÍR FIACHRACH
Tireragh

TITLE: *1840, p.31:* Tyreragh. Index, p.VI: Tír Fhiachraigh. Tune: *1840, p.31.*

NOTES

This tune was taken down from "an old man at Sligo in 1802" (Index, p.XI). There is no MS. copy.

The name of the place, under any form of spelling, is not in the *Townland Index*. But Hogan's *Onomasticon Goedelicum* (1910), which is a great standard work, lists *Tír Fiachrach Mhuaidhe* as the barony of Tirerah in County Sligo. This is doubtless the place from which the tune took its title.

41. PLANXTY BURKE

TITLE: *1840, p.31:* Plangsty Burke. By Carolan. Index, p.V: Plangstae Bhuair-
cidh. Tune: *DOSC*, I, p.172. [This is copied from Thompson's *Hibernian Muse*
(c.1786) p.63.]

NOTES
This tune,, for which there are no words, was noted by Bunting
from Charles Byrne the harper in 1802. Hardiman (*Irish Minstrelsy*,
1831, p.VII) states that Planxty Bourke "was composed by Carolan
for a member of a respectable family of that name near Castlebar" (County Mayo). If so, the subject is probably Thomas Burke,
who represented the Borough of Castlebar in King James's Irish
Parliament of 1689, and for whom Carolan wrote another piece
(cf. *DOSC* I p.172, and *DOSC* II p.12: also *DOSB* III p.62/63).

[The tune is also found in the following collections:
   Neale's *Celebrated Irish Tunes* (c.1726) p.21 *Collection of Carolan
      Tunes* (post 1743) p.10 (no flat in key signature)
   Lee's *Favourite Collection* (c.1780) p.27
   Thompson's *Hibernian Muse* (c.1786) p.63

O'Neill's *Music of Ireland* (1903) No.664 — copied from *Bunting 1840*

Mulholland's *Ancient Irish Airs* (1810) p.79 (Planxty McDermot).
There is a version in the Bunting MSS. (MS.33, bk.2, p.48) which is almost identical to the *1840* tune, and is marked "out of printed book, part of this air from Charles Byrne". There is a copy of this version in MS.33, bk.5, p.58.]

42. DRUIMIN DUBH
The Black Cow

TITLE: *1840, p.32:* Druimin dubh — Dear black cow. Index, p.III: Drinmin dubh. Tune: MS.29, p.132/3 and MS.33, bk.2, p.22.

D'éirigh mé amach ar maidin Dia Domhnaigh,
Is fuair mé mo dhruimin dubh báidhte i bpoll móna.
Ghread mé mo bhasa 'gus leig mé na gártha,
Ar shúil go ndéanfadh sé an druimin dubh beó dhom.

Ó rú, 'dhruimin dubh, Ó 'rú 'ghradh,
Ó rú, 'dhruimin dubh, dílis bhreagh!
Ó rú, 'dhruimin dubh, Ó 'rú 'ghradh,
Ó 'dhruimin dubh dílis, go dtí tú slán!

Ní dheachaigh aon bhuarach suas ar chois
An bhó bha chomhsamhla leis an Ghlais.
'Sí ba mhó bainne 'gus ba mhilse blas,
Mo bhrón chreach maidne ní fhéadaim a leas!

TRANSLATION
1. I got up on Sunday morning, And found my black cow drowned in a bog-hole. I wrung my hands and cried aloud, In the hope that my black cow would become alive. Refrain: Ó rú, black cow, órú my love, Ó rú, dear lovely black cow! Ó rú, black cow, órú my love, Ó! dear black cow, may you be safe! 2. No spancel ever went on the leg of the cow that was the image of the Glas. It is she gave abundant milk of the sweetest taste, My deep morning grief that I shall not have her benefit!

NOTE
"Noted from Arthur O'Neill, Harper, 1800" (Index, p.VIII). The above tune is based on a very rough notation in MS.29 and has been reconstructed from two MS. versions. The comparison of the cow with the Glas in verse 2 needs explanation. The Glas-Ghaibhlinn was a celebrated cow in Irish mythology, going back for centuries. Its fame was due to the fact that it could never by fully milked.

[In the *1840* Volume, Bunting gives a translation of the words under the tune. On p.93 of the Introduction he translates three verses of a political song to the same tune where the Druimin Dubh represents "by a very whimsical metaphor, the cause of the exiled monarch". In Hardiman's *Irish Minstrelsy*, Volume II, p.145 the Irish original of Bunting's translation on p.93, is to be found. The words are also to be found in MS.11, p.26 and in MS.17 with a translation.]

EDWARD BUNTING

Facsimile from Bunting's Notebook.

43. THE BANKS OF CLAUDY

TITLE: *1840, p.33, No.43:* Banks of Claudy. Index, p.II: Bruach an Chladaigh.
Tune: MS.33, bk.2, p.67 "Banks of Claudy or Plain of Boccarough." "From
Charles Byrne.

As I roved out one evening, being in the month of May,
Down by the sally garden I carelessly did stray.
I overheard a young maid in sorrow to complain
All for her absent lover, and Johnny was his name.

I stepped up to this young girl, I took her by surprise
I'd own she did not know me, I being in disguise,
Said I "My pretty fair maid, my joy and heart's delight,
Tell me how far you've travelled this dark and weary night."

"Kind sir, the road to Claudy would you be pleased to show
Take pity on a fair one who knows not where to go.
I'm in search of a faithless young man, and Johnny is his name,
Sure it's on the Banks of Claudy I'm told he does remain.

"This is the Banks of Claudy, the ground whereon you stand,
Do not depend on Johnny, for he's a false young man.
Do not depend on Johnny, he will not meet you here
But tarry with me in these green woods, no danger need you fear."

"Oh! if my Johnny were here this night, he'd keep me safe from harm
But he's on the field of battle, all in his unform.
He's on the field of battle and his foes he does defy
Like a ruling prince of honour near to the walls of Troy."

"It's about six months or better since your Johnny left the shore
He's sailing on the ocean, where the foaming billows roar.
He's sailing on the ocean, for honour and bright fame.
As I'm told the ship was lost going round the coasts of Spain."

Oh! when she heard this dreadful news she could no longer stand,
To the tearing of her golden hair and the wringing of her hands
"Then since my Johnny's drowned no other man I'll take,
Through lonesome dales and valleys I'll wander for his sake."

Then when I saw her loyalty I could no longer stand,
I took her in my arms, saying "Betty, I'm your man!
I'm your true and constant Johnny, the cause of all your pain,
And since we met at Claudy we'll never part again!"

NOTES

AIR: There is a rough second copy in MS.29, p.3, with no indication of origin. In MS.33, bk.2, p.67 (above) Bunting writes the following underneath the tune: "This is the same air as 'Cailín Donn' in the first volume." (*1796 Collection*, p.18, No.32). [There is an obvious relationship between the latter and the MS. version of 'The Banks of Claudy' (above). The disparity between the MS. version and the *1840* published version of the tune is possibly explained by the fact that the former was noted from Charles Byrne (no date given) while the latter was noted from Hugh Higgins in 1792. However, the MS. tune above, needs to be reconstructed if the words are to fit it. This can be done logically and effectively by re-arranging the various phrases of the tune into the form abb¹ a¹ which is the form of its variant 'An Cailín Donn'. The reconstructed tune (see below) is now a perfect vehicle for the words.]

WORDS: Copied from Henry's *Songs of the People*, vol. iii, No. 693. The note on the broadsheet is as follows: "This is the premier ballad of Ireland. It is sung all over the Green Isle and each district has its own variations. This version is from the Faughan Vale (County Londonderry) and though sung in the cottage came to hand from the castle." Claudy is a village on the right bank of the Faughan, a small stream which rises in the Sperrin mountains and joins the River Foyle just before it enters Lough Foyle in County Londonderry.

[Another version of the song (words and music) is to be found in *Folksongs sung in Ulster* by Robin Morton (Cork, 1970). In *Folk song in England* A.L. Lloyd mentions (p.32) that 'the Banks of Claudy' has turned up "in Sussex and Scotland, Virginia, U.S.A., and Victoria, Australia, practically word-for-word the same and we have to presume that these versions have probably come from, and been more or less fixed by, some printed original on a broadside or in a popular songster".

In MS.5, p.39 there is variant of the 'Banks of Claudy' under the title 'Portaferry Boys'.

In the notes to the song 'My Singing Bird' in *Four Irish Songs* (p.15), C. Milligan-Fox writes: "The melody to which the words were written was taken down from William Simpson of Moneyrea, one of the few remaining handloom weavers in Co. Down. He played it upon the fiddle and called it 'The Bank of Claudy'." There is no obvious connection, however, between the two tunes.

In the Introduction (p.98) to the *1840* volume, Bunting writes the following: "Banks of Claudy. Interesting for its peculiar bass accompaniment which was taken down from the harper nearly as it is here given." The MS. copy on which the *1840* version was based is in MS.29, p.3 with no key or time signature and with a bass included. Page 4 of the MS., however, begins with a different piece and the fragment which survives is given below. A comparison of both basses shows how Bunting's published version is mostly his own arrangement, while at the same time being influenced to some extent by the MS.29 bass.]

44. SIR FESTUS BURKE

TITLE: *1840, p.34:* Sir Festus Burke. Index, *1840,* p.IV: Fiacha a Burc. Tune: MS.33, bk.3, pp.46/7.

NOTES

The source of this tune is MS.33, bk.3, pp.46-7: "Sir Festus Burke, by Carolan." It was noted by Bunting from Charles Fannin, the harper, in 1792 and is published in my edition of Carolan, Vol. I, p.170, with notes in Vol. II, pp.9-10. No words are extant.

Sir Festus Burke (in Irish, Fiach de Búrca) was the 5th Baronet of Glinsk, County Galway, succeeding to the title on the death of his father, Sir John Burke, 4th Baronet, on the 4th July, 1721. The latter was the half-brother of Sir Ulick Burke, 3rd Baronet, for whom Carolan composed a song of six verses in Irish (I, p.169 and II, p.8 in my edition).

Sir Festus married Lady Laetitia, eldest daughter of the Earl of Clanricard, but there were no children of the marriage, which took place in 1708. He died in 1730 and his wife survived him by about ten years, dying on the 29th June, 1740.

45. MISS MacDERMOTT or THE PRINCESS ROYAL

TITLE: *1840, p.35:* The Princess Royal. By Carolan. Index, p.II: Beanphrionsa Rioghamhuil. Tune: MS.5, p.62 (printed in *DOSC* I, p.210).

NOTES

There is a close variant noted by Coady in MS.6, p.35.

From Arthur O'Neill in 1800. In his Introduction to *1840*, p.99, Bunting states (doubtless on the authority of O'Neill) that this tune was "composed by Carolan for the daughter of MacDermott Roe, the representative of the old princes of Coolavin". This somewhat vague statement is discussed in my edition of Carolan, Vol.II, pp.50 and 52 without any definite conclusion being reached as to the identity of the subject; and as there are no extant words we receive no help in that direction. There are two branches of this Roscommon family, the MacDermotts of Alderford, who are usually distinguished by the title of MacDermott Roe, and the MacDermotts of Coolavin. It was the head of the latter that was known in Carolan's time, and even later, as the Prince of Coolavin. It seems probable, therefore, that the lady known as the Princess Royal was his eldest daughter and not, as stated by Bunting, a daughter of MacDermott Roe.

"The Princess Royal" is one of the most celebrated of Carolan's compositions, largely because of its association with the words of the song "The Arethusa", to which it was set by Shield towards the end of the eighteenth century. The printed history of the air is extensively reviewed in the *Musical Times* for October, 1894 by that first-class scholar the late Dr. Frank Kidson. From this it appears that the earliest printed copies are in Walsh's *Compleat Country Dancing Master* (c.1730), entitled "The Princess Royal, the new way"; and an oblong quarto of about the same date in the Wighton Collection in Dundee Public Library, "Princess Royal". The earliest printed attribution to Carolan is in O'Farrell's *Pocket Companion*, book IV (c.1810), where the title is simply "Air by Carolan. Irish". But the ascription to him in the MS. copy from which the tune is printed above is some years earlier than this, and it has the tradition of the harpers behind it.

The song of "The Arethusa" originally appeared in a small opera or musical entertainment called "The Lock and Key", which was acted in 1796. Shield was responsible for the musical side, and the libretto was by Prince Hoare. The popularity of this particular number was helped by the anti-French feeling of the time. It chronicles an engagement between the "Arethusa" (Captain Marshall) and the frigate "La Belle Poule" in the English Channel, 17th June, 1778:

On deck five hundred men did dance,
The stoutest they could find in France:
We with two hundred did advance
    On board of the Arethusa.
Our captain hailed the Frenchman, 'Ho!'
The Frenchman then cried out 'Hallo!' —
'Bear down, d'ye see, to our Admiral's lee.'
'No, no,' says the Frenchman, 'that can't be.' —
'Then I must lug you along with me,'
    Says the saucy Arethusa.

[In the printed version Bunting raises the 6th and 7th notes of the scale for harmonic reasons in bars 6 and 18.

Apart from the references to the tune listed in *DOSC* II, p.52, it also appears under the title "Brian the Brave" in the *Journal of the Irish Folk Song Society*, Vol.XII, p.17.

The tune is still played today as a set dance called "Rodney's Glory" (see O'Neill's *Dance Music of Ireland*, No.958). The set dance gets its name from a set of verses written to the tune by the poet Eoghain Rua Ó Súilleabháin in the year 1782 to commemorate a naval battle between forces under Rodney, then vice-Admiral of Great Britain and De Grasse, the French Admiral. This battle took place in 1782, four years after the 'Arethusa' engagement mentioned above. (See *Amhráin Eoghain Ruaidh Uí Shúilleabháin* by Dineen, p.XVII et seq.) A jig variant of the tune may be found in *Ceol Rince na hÉireann*, Vol. I, No.22 under the title "Port Shean tSeáin".]

46. GRÁINNE MHAOL
Granuile

TITLE: *1840, p.36:* Granu Weal or Ma, Ma, Ma. Index, p.IV: Gráine Mhaol.
Tune: MS.33, bk.2, p.59: origin unstated.

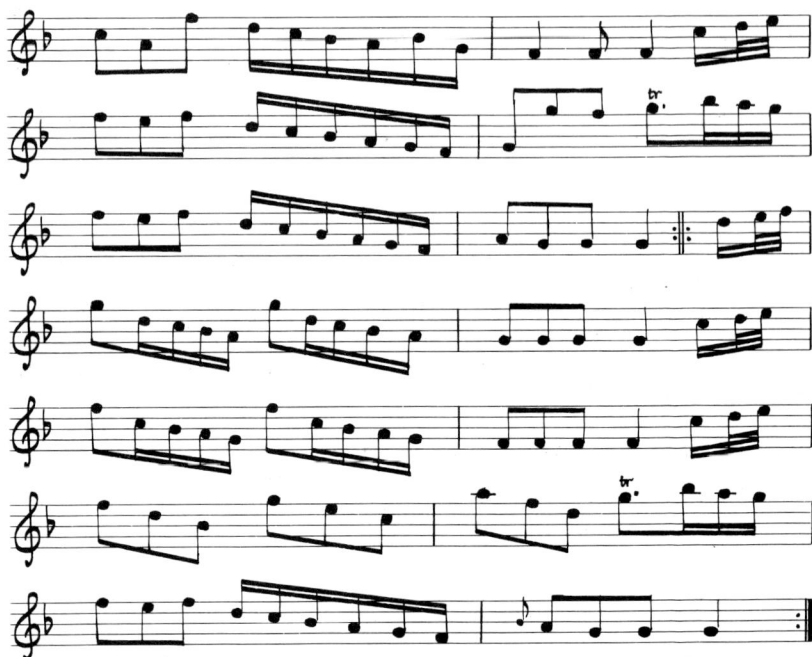

Is baintreabhach bhocht dheacrach í Gráinne Mhaol
Ó sgar sí le spalpaire an áidh 's a' tséin.
Dá dtagadh faoi bhaile bheadh báire léi,
Is bheadh macnaois mhaith againn le fagháil sa' réim.

Mo lagar! Is leanbh dhá clainn bhocht mé,
'S nach bhfuil ceart ar bith agam le fagháil, faraoir!
Na baclaigh nár bhuain dóibh bheith teann sa' réim
Bheith macnaois ar leabaidh lem' mháithrín féin.

Ná bíodh buaireadh ort, a stuadh-bhean na meang 's na seád,
Óir chualaidh an gruagach do chlann bheith i bpéin.
Gluaiseam glan-uaibhreach le lán-cheart tréan,
'Tabhairt fuascailt ón chluanaidh do Ghráinne Mhaol.

Beidh saoithe go suaimhneach ar chlár cheart Gaedhil,
Beidh fíonta dhá spíonadh ar dháimh 's ar éigs'
Beidh an chaoinchruit aríst linn ar chlár go séimh,
'S beidh a caointeach go h-aoibhinn le Gráinne Mhaol.

TRANSLATION

1. A poor wretched widow is Granuaile, Since she was parted from the prosperous happy warrior. If he should return home she would be the victor, And there would be good times, happiness and ease in the realm. 2. My weakness! I am a child of her poor family, And I can obtain no right whatever, alas! The crowd that have no claim to be established in the realm Are at ease in bed

74

with my own mother. 3. Be not troubled, stately lady of the smiles(?) and the jewels, For the warrior has heard that your children are oppressed. Let us march full proudly with a strong sense of right, To bring deliverance to those pastures (?) of Granuaile. 4. The sages will be tranquil on the true plain of the Gael, Wines will be flowing for poets and bards, The gentle harp will be with us again on a graceful table, And the menacing foreigner will be well-disposed to Granuaile.

NOTES

AIR: According to the Index of *1840*, Bunting's tune was noted from "MacDonnell the piper in 1797". The alternative title is explained in the Intro. (p.93): "When played on the pipes, the tune at intervals is made to have a peculiar sound, which has procured it the additional name of 'Ma, Ma, Ma,' ". In the MSS. the tune is followed by two sets of variations.

[Bunting includes E flat in the signature of the *1840* version and also uses an F sharp for harmonic reasons. The following is a list of the occurrences of the tune in various collections:
Cookes *Selection of 21 Irish Airs* (1793) — This seems to be the eariest reference.
O'Farrell's *Pocket Companion for the Irish or Union Pipes* (1801-10), Volume IV, p.99: — a variant of Cooke.
O'Daly's *Poets and Poetry of Munster*, Volume II, p.92/93. The text only is given and the reader is referred to O'Farrell's *Pocket Companion* for the tune.
Stanford Petrie, No. 1455: — a variant of Cooke.
The tune in Cooke is 12 bars in length and one verse of the text takes up 8 bars. The last four. bars are a repeat of the middle four in the manner of a chorus.
The tune in O'Farrell has 8 bars in the first section and 9 bars in the second section. If bars 13 and 14 are combined by changing the notes in both bars to quavers, the tune becomes symmetrical and two verses of the text fit it played once through.
Bunting's tune, being a piper's version is unsuitable for singing and Cooke's version is without doubt the most suitable for fitting the text to.]

WORDS: Bunting MS.7, No.151.
These differ from the song of the same name written to the tune by the poet Seán Clárach MacDomhnaill (1691-1751) and are doubtless older. Hardiman (in *Irish Minstrelsy*, p.143, Vol.II) prints what he claims are the original words.
For more than a century, "Granuaile" has come to mean Ireland in patriotic songs, like three or four other female names, such as "Kathleen Ní Houlihan", which is the title of a play by W.B. Yeats. But unlike these others, Granuaile was a real person. She lived at Carrigahooly Castle, which is at an inlet in the bay of Newport,

Co. Mayo. Volume II of *Anthologia Hibernica* (July 1793) begins with an engraving of "Carrigahooly Castle", followed by an article entitled "an account of Grana Uile's Castle". It begins by stating that "Grace O'Maly, known among the Irish by the name of Grana Uile, lived at Carrick a owly, at an inlet in the bay of Newport". It continues:

"She was the daughter of Owen O'Mally and widow of O'Flaherty, two Irish chiefs in those parts. After the death of the last, she married Sir Richard Bourke, styled MacWilliam Eighter (son of William junior) who died in 1585 after having by her three sons and one daughter." She "accompanied her father and his sept in many naval expeditions. The coast was plundered of cattle and other property. . . . But the English power growing stronger in Connaught, she resolved to make her peace with Queen Elizabeth and went to her court." The interview had to be conducted through an interpreter as Grace knew no English.

"The Queen, surrounded by her ladies, received her in great state. Grana was introduced in the dress of her country: a long mantle covered her head and body; her hair was gathered on her crown and fastened with a bodkin; her breast was bare, and she had a yellow bodice and petticoat. The court stared at her with surprise at so strange a figure, when one of the ladies perceived that Grace wanted a pocket handkerchief, which was instantly handed to her. After she had used it she threw it into the fire. Another was given her, and she was told by an interpreter that it was to be put in her pocket. Grace felt indignant at this intimation and applying it to her nose threw it into the fire, declaring that in her country they were much cleanlier than to pocket what came from their nostrils. After having made her peace, she returned to Ireland and landed in a little creek near Hoath [Howth.]"

47. THE PIPERS DANCE

TITLE: *1840, p.36:* Kiss me Lady. Index, p.V: Raince Píobaire; The Piper's Dance. Tune: *1840*, p.36.

NOTES

[Collected from "Macdonnell the piper in 1797". This is a variant of the popular folk song entitled "Tá dhá gabhairín buí agam". The tune is hexatonic with the seventh missing. The title at the head of the piece is different from that given in the Index. In the notes to tune No. 110, "An Gabhairín Buí", in *Ceol Rinnce na hÉireann*, Cuid 2, (p.171), Breandán Breathnach lists variants with the following titles: Hielan Laddie; The Bonnie Lass of Livingston; Cockle Shells; and The High Cauled Cap.]

48. TAKE MY LOVE UNTO THE YOUNG MAN

TITLE: *1840, p.37:* Take my love. *1840, p.II:* Beir mo ghrádh — Take my love to that young man. Tune: MS.5, p.80: "From J. McC. Take my love unto the young man."

NOTES

The Index (p.X) states that the piece was noted from " J. Mc Cracken, Esq. Moneymore". The tune is also in MS.33, bk.5, p.55, with a bass added and marked "Vivace".

77

49. (and 121) SÍLE BHEAG NÍ CHONNALLÁIN
Little Celia Connellan

TITLE: *1840, p.37:* "Celia Connallon". *1840, p.91:* "Celia Connallon – Second Set". Index, p.V: Sheala Ní Chonalláin. Index, p.V: Sheela Beg Ní Chonallaín. Tune: MS.33, bk.3, p.9 – "from Donal Black's singing and also from Charles Byrne".

A Shíle bhán na bpéarlaí,
   A chéad-shearc nár fhullaing gruaim,
D'fhág tú m'intinn buartha,
   Is id' dhiaidh-se ní bheidh mé buan.
Muna dtigidh tú do mfhéachain
   Is éalódh liom fá ghleanntaibh cuain,
Beidh cumha is tuirse id' dhéidh orm,
   Is beidh mé chomh dubh le gual!

Tugthar chughainn na fíonta,
   Agus líontar dhúinn an ghloine is fearr,
Muna bhfaghad féin cead sínte
   Le mín-chneis a bhrollaigh bháin.
A phlúir is gile 's is míne
   Ná an síoda 's ná clúmh na n-éan,
Is buaidheartha tuirseach bhím-se
   Nuair smaoinighim bheith 'scaramhaint léi!

Dá mbeinn-se féin is mín-chneas,
   Caoin-mhéar an bhrollaigh bhreágh,
I ngleanntán aoibhinn aereach
   Ó thuitim oidhche go n-éireóchadh lá,
Gan neach a bheith dhár gcoimhdeacht
   Acht cearca-fraoigh nó'n coileach feadha,
'S go mbíodh greann gan cham im' chroidhe 'stigh
   Do Shíle Ní Chonnalláin!

78

1. Fair Celia of the pearly teeth, O dearest love that banished gloom, You have left my mind troubled, And without you I shall not live for long. Unless you come to see me And steal away with me through the winding valleys, Loneliness and anguish will afflict me, And I shall be black as coal. 2. Let wines be given us, And let the best drinking-glass be filled for us, Unless I am allowed to lie with the slender skin of her fair bosom. O flower that is whiter and softer Than silk or than the feathers of birds 'Tis troubled and weary I am When I think of being parted from her. 3. Would that I were with the fair-skinned girl, Tender-fingered lass of the lovely bosom, In a delightful airy valley From night-fall till the dawn of day, With nobody in our company Save heather-hens or pheasant, And there would be love unrestrained inside my heart For Celia Connellan.

NOTES
AIR: [It would appear from the Index p.VII that No.49 was collected from Arthur O'Neill the harper in 1792 while No.121 (the second set) was collected from Charles Byrne the harper in the same year. This could account for the two versions of the tune. Certainly No.121 (MS. version above) which was also collected from 'Donal Black's singing' is a singable version while No.49 has the marks of a harp version. The Index p.VII states that Thomas Connallon composed the piece in 1660 while the date 1650 is given at the head of both printed versions. A list of references to the tune in various collections can be found in *DOSB* VI, p.52. Two more versions of the tune are to be found in Joyce's 1909 collection, p.306. These were taken from the *Forde MS.*]

WORDS: There are three verses in MS.10, No.39 entitled "Síle Ní Chonallan"; but they are very poor and could only with difficulty be sung to the tune. Hence I have substituted the version in Edward Walsh's *Irish Popular Songs* (1847) p.98. Bunting omits the word "bheag" (little) from his printed title; but it is in his MS. and also in Walsh.

50. WHY SHOULD NOT POOR FOLK?

TITLE: *1840, p.38:* Why should not poor folk. Index, p.II: Cad fath nach ndéinfadh na boicht? Tune: MS.33, bk.2, p.68.

NOTES

Bunting states (*1840*, p.98) that this tune "was noted down by the Editor, in the year 1792, from the performance of an old man well known by the "soubriquet" of "Poor Folk", who formerly perambulated the northern counties, playing on a tin fiddle". [In the Index, p.XI he gives the date of collection as 1807.] Actually it is merely an extended version of "A ghaoith ón nDeas" ("O Wind from the South"), published in Bunting's *1809* volume, p.37. [Details of the latter are in *DOSB* V, p.29 et seq.]

51. GET UP EARLY

TITLE: *1840, p.39:* Get up early. Index, p.VI: Youghall duishi. Tune: MS.33, bk.2, p.44. The key signature has two flats, but the *E* is raised throughout.

NOTES

According to the Index of *1840*, Bunting noted the tune from Richard Stanton of Westport, County Mayo, in 1802. The MS. however mentions the placename of Ballinrobe.

The first part of the tune is a close variant of the well-known double jig, "The Rakes of Kildare", which appears in numerous collections of Irish dance music. It was first printed as such in Levey's *Dance Music of Ireland* (1858), where it is simply called "A jig". [The tune is also a variant of the song 'Fágaimid siúd mar atá sé' which can be found in Joyce's *"Ancient Music of Ireland"* (1873), p.13/14, and also in MS.33, bk.4, p.24 of the Bunting MSS. O'Neill refers to the tune in *Irish Folk Music*, p.139, and also in *Irish Minstrels and Musicians*, p.132 where he points out its relationship with the hornpipe "The First of May".]

52. TÁ CRANN AR AN gCOILL
There is a Tree in the Wood

TITLE: *1840, p.40:* The tree in the wood. Index, p.III: Crann ar an choill.
Tune: MS.33, bk.I, p.3.

Tá crann ar an gcoill agus is úire ar a dtagann a bhláth,
Is ag tíocht don tsamhradh is binn guth cuaiche 'n-a bharr.
Arís ins a' geimhreadh an t-am dtuiteann a bhláth,
Bíonn na géagáin lom 's a' londubh ag iarraidh sgáith.

A mháthair na páirt', ná trácht ar a léithide siúd,
Agus le h-áirnéis gránda go bráth ná mealltar thú.
Nuair a bhíos an cnuasóigín gránda i gclabar go dtí na glún,
Beidh coiscéim stáideamhail árd ag géag na lúb.

TRANSLATION

1. There's a tree in the wood and more freshly come its blossoms, And when summer comes, sweet is the cuckoo's voice atop of it. Again in the winter, the time when its blossom falls, The branches are bare and the blackbird is seeking shelter. 2. Beloved mother, don't talk of the like, And by ugly wealth never be enticed. When the ugly stumpish woman(?) is up to her knees in mud, The branch of the curls (?) will have a stately tread.

NOTES

Both air and words were noted in 1802 from blind Redmond Stanton of Westport, Co. Mayo (Index, p.XI). [Another version of the words are to be found in *Dhá Chéad de Cheoltaibh Uladh* by Énrí Ó Muirghéasa, p.153.] The two verses seem to be unrelated and probably belong to different songs.

The tune is one of a number of airs used for folk-songs in this meter, the most celebrated being "Bean an fhir ruaidh" (The Red-haired Man's Wife).

53. CAILÍN DEAS DONN
A Pretty Brown-Haired Maid

TITLE: *1840, p.40:* 'Pretty Brown Maid'. Index, p.III: Cailín deas donn. Tune: MS.33, bk.2, p.53.

[Collected at "Deel Castle, Ballina in 1792" (Index p.IX). The MS. states that it was collected "from Charles Byrne. Also called 'Bobby in Bed' ". The MS. version is in the Dorian mode while the published version is an Ionian tune. Both versions are curiously related in that the latter is almost an exact mirror of the former transposed down one step but with the same key signature. Whether both are genuine tunes collected from different sources or whether the *1840* version is the result of Bunting's attempt at improving the tune, it is not possible to say. A somewhat similar example may be seen in the relationship between two well known reels at the present time, "My Love is in America" and "The Dunmore Lasses". For printed versions of these see O'Neill's *Dance Music of Ireland*, No. 586, and Breathnach's *Ceol Rince na hÉireann*, Vol. I, No.189.]

54. NA GAMHNA GEALA
The Lovely Calves

TITLE: *1840, p.41:* The White Calf. Index, p.IV: Gamhna Geala. Tune: *1840*, p.41.

Siad mo chuid gamhna na gamhna geal,
Itheann siad a' féar is ní ólann siad a' bainne.
Gabhann siad anonn is anall ar a' mBanna,
'S ní fearr leó a' tráigh aca ná an lán mara.

Is beag mo bheinn ar thigheach ceann-slátaigh,
Ar fhuinneóga gloine nó ar leapacha árda.
Ceólta na cruinne 's iad dá seinnim in mo chluasa —
Ba bhinne liom-sa géimneach na ngamhna sa' mbuailigh.

Bheirim mo mhallacht don tsagart a phós mé,
Nó don té a d'órdaigh na bailte móra.
Ba mhíle b'fhearr liom-sa bothóg lá samhraidh,
Poll bheith ar a' sgraith 's mé ag amharc ar na gamhna.

Níor bhfearr liom clúmhach fúm ná luachair,
'S níor bhfearr liom raibhín orm ná buarach.
Níor bhfearr liom ar hallaibh is iad a bheith buailte,
Nó poll a bheith ar a lantaoir 's mé ag amharc ar a' mbuailigh.

TRANSLATION

1. 'Tis my own calves are the lovely calves, They eat the grass and they don't drink the milk. They go to and fro on the [river] Bann, And they don't prefer the strand to the full tide. 2. 'Tis little I care for houses with slated roofs, For glass windows or for beds off the floor. If the melodies of the world were ringing in my ears, Sweeter to me would be the lowing of the calves in the milking field. 3. I send my curse to the priest who married me, Or to the man who arranged for the large towns. I would rather a thousand times a cottage on a summer's day, With a hole in the green sods [of the wall] and I looking at the calves. I would not prefer down feathers under me to rushes, I would not prefer a ribbon to a spancel, I would not prefer . . . .(?) To a hole in the lantern for me to watch the calves.

NOTES

Collected "at Deel Castle, Ballina in 1792" (Index, p.XI). [In the published tune Bunting raises the note B flat occasionally, presumably for harmonic reasons. This has been corrected in the above copy and the tune is restored to its original aeolian mode. Bunting repeated the last phrase in the tune and this presents a problem when setting the words. There is either a two line chorus missing from the words or else Bunting himself repeated the last phrase of the tune merely for effect. There may be a relationship between this song and "Ailliliú Na nGamhna" in Walshe's *Ceol Ár Sinsear*, p.88.

The MS. version is in MS.33, bk.3, p.49 with a figured bass and is marked "From Charles Byrne's Singing". It is virtually identical to the *1840* version, including the raised notes, but with a key signature of four sharps. Another copy of the words is to be found in MS.25, p.5.]

55. THE REJECTED LOVER

TITLE: *1840, p.41:* The Rejected Lover. Index, p.I, An Graidheóir Diultadhaé.
Tune: *1840*, p.41: The Rejected Lover.

Her hair was like the beaten gold
Or like a spider's spinning.
It was in her you might behold
My joys and woes beginning.

Then since you hate my low estate,
Bad luck will sure go with you.
I never more will darken your door
To tell how much I love you.

But since you're free in telling me
You're in no haste to marry,
I'll be as free in telling thee
I care not how long you tarry.

NOTES

The air which was noted in 1792 from Dr. William Stokes, is not in
these MSS. The words are on a loose sheet between pages 37 and 38
of MS.12, No.1. I know of no other source for either air or words.
There are verses entitled "The Rejected Lover" on a broadsheet
in Henry's *Songs of the People*, Vol.2, No.589, but they are in a
different metre and could not be sung to Bunting's tune. [In the
Intro. p.100, Bunting writes: "This air varies from the other melodies
in the collection in the extreme shortness of its phrases. The repe-
tition of the note in the first and second bars at the beginning of
the second part and also at the end of the tune is a characteristic
trait in Irish music."

This air was set by Stanford with words by A.P. Graves, beginning
"In Innisfallen's Fairy Isle".]

56. BALLINDERRY

TITLE: *1840, p.42:* Ballinderry and Cronán. Index, p.III: Cronán. Tune: MS. 33, bk.5, pp. 12/13. Music with the first verse is written under the notes.

WORDS: *1840*, p.42

It's pretty to be in Ballinderry,
It's pretty to be in Agahlee,
It's prettier to be in bonny Ram's Island,
Sitting under an Ivy tree.

Ochón ochón, ochón ochón.

Oh! that I was in little Ram's Island,
Oh! that I was with Phelimy Diamond;
He would whistle and I would sing,
Till we would make the whole Island ring.

Ochón ochón, ochón ochón.

NOTES

Both air and words were collected from Dr. Crawford of Lisburn, in 1808. Another version of the words, from Mrs. Houston, was printed in the *Journal of the Irish Folk song Society*, Vol.V, (1907), p.37. It runs as follows:

  O, it's purty to be in the bonny Church Island,
  Nobody there but Phelim my diamond;
  Phelim would whistle and I would sing,
  Until we would make Church Island to ring.

86

Phelimy, Phelimy, why did you leave me?
Sure I could bake, I could sew I could spin.
Phelimy, Phelimy, why did you leave me,
I'll tell the priest on you Phelimy, Phil.

O, lonely I wander on bonny Church Island
Far, far away from Phelimy diamond
The birds may whistle a merry tune,
But sorrowful May brought woeful June.

Och, cold in the ground my Phelim's lying,
Over his grave I am sobbing, I'm sighing
To leave him his love would be a sin,
So take off the sod and lay me in.

Ballinderry is on the edge of a small lake which is very close to
Lough Neagh, which is the largest lake in Ireland; and Aghalee is
just south of Ballinderry.
There is a copy of the tune with six Irish verses in *Cláirseach na
nGaedheal*, part III, 1903, the origin of the words is not stated.
[On p.88 of the Intro. Bunting makes the following comment:
"The crónán or chorus will be found to form a tolerably perfect
bass, except in the last bar, which wants the cadence to make it
complete."]

57. AN SPAILÍN FÁNACH *or* THE GIRL I LEFT BEHIND ME

TITLE: *1840, p.43:* The girl I left behind me. Index p.II: An Spailpin Fanach.
Tune: MS.33, Bk.5, p.24.

NOTES

Noted from Arthur O'Neill, Harper, 1800 (Index, p.X).

In the last century, this tune was equally well known in Ireland as "An Spailín Fánach" and in both England and Ireland as "The Girl I left behind me". Thomas Moore's song "As slow our ship" was written to it; and Alfred Moffat has the following note to this song in his *Minstrelsy of Ireland*, p.14:

"Mr. Chappell claims this lively air as English, and informs us that it occurs in a manuscript of about 1770 belonging to Dr. Rimbault, as 'The girl I left behind me; or Brighton Camp.' Mr. Chappell considers that this refers to the encampments along the coast in 1758-9 when admirals Hawke and Rodney were watching the French fleet. All this may be true enough, but by no means proves that the air was not originally imported from Ireland. It has a decidedly Irish flavour about it, and in many ways resembles that undoubtedly Irish melody, known as "The Rose tree in full bearing". Moore's verses were written in the autumn of 1817, and published in the following year in the seventh number of the *Melodies*; his version of the air is singularly incorrect. Bunting's setting, given in his work of 1840, and which he informs us was obtained from 'A. O'Niel, harper' in 1800 is a mere parody on the genuine air."

I first give "An Spailpín Fánach" (which means "The Wandering Harvest Labourer") as printed in O'Daly's *Poets and Poetry of Munster* (Second Series, 1860), p.77, with a metrical translation by "Erionnach, M.D.", who was the late Dr. George Sigerson.

Go deó deó arís ní raghad go Caiseal
    Ag díol 'n-a éic mo shláinte,
Ná ar mharagadh na saoire im' shuidhe cois balla
    Im' scaoinse ar leat-taoibh sráide:
Bodairidhe na tíre a' tígheacht ar a gcapaill,
    Dá fhiafraidhe an bhfuilim hírálta —
Téanam chum siubhail, tá'n cúrsa fada,
    Seo ar siubhal an Spailpín Fánach!

Im Spailpín Fánach fágadh mise,
    Ag seasamh ar mo shláinte,
Ag siubhal an drúchta go moch ar maidin,
    'S ag bailiughadh galair ráithche!
Ní fheicfear corán im' láimh chum bainte,
    Súist ná feac bheag rámhainne,
Acht *colours* na bhFranncach ós cionn mo leapthan,
    Is *pike* agam chum sáidhte!

88

Go Callainn nuair théighim 's mo *hook* im' ghlaic,
    'S mé annsúd i dtosach geárrtha;
'S nuair théighim go Duibhlinn 'sé clú bhíonn aca,
    Seo chughaibh an Spailpín Fánach!
Cruinnéochadh mé ciall is triallfad abhaile,
    Is claoidhfead seal lem' mháithrín,
'S go bráth arís ní ghlaodhfar m'ainim
    San tír seo "An Spailpín Fánach!"

Mo chúig céad slán chum dúthaighe m'athar,
    Agus chum an Oileáin ghrádhmhar,
'S chum buachaillí na Cúlach, ó's díobh nár mhisde
    I n-aimsir chasda na gárdan.
Ach anois ó táim-se im' chaidhin bhocht dhealbh
    I measc na ndúthaighe fághain seo,
Is é mo chumha croidhe mar fuair mé an ghairm
    Bheith ariamh im' Spailpín Fánach!

I gCiarraighe an ghrinn do gheobhthaoi an ainnir
    Go m'fhonn le fear suidhe láimh léi,
'N-a mbeidh lasa trí lítis 'n-a gnaoi mar eala,
    'S a cúl fionn fada fáinneach;
A cruinne chíocha 'riamh nár scaipeadh,
    'S a mala chaol mar shnáithe;
Is mór go mb'fhearr liom í ná sraoill ó Challainn
    'N-a mbeidh na céadta púnt le fághail léi!

Is ró-bhreágh is cuimhin liom mo dhaoine bheith sealad
    Thair ag Droichead Gháile,
Faoi bhuaibh, faoi chaoire, faoi laoigh beag geala,
    'Gus capaill ann le n-áireamh.
B'é toil Chríosd gurd cuireach sinn asda,
    'S go ndeachamair a leath ár sláinte;
'S gurb' é bhris mo chroidhe i ngach tír dá rachaim,
    "*Call here, you* Spailpín Fánach!"

Dá dtigeadh an Franncach anall thar Chaladh,
    'S a champa daingean, láidir,
Agus Boic Ó Gráda chughainn abhaile,
    Is Tadhg bocht fiall Ó Dálaigh,
Do bheadh *Barracks* an rígh go léir dá leagadh,
    Agus *yeoman* againn dá gcárna,
Clanna Gaoidhil gach am dá dtreasgairt —
    Sin cabhair ag an Spailpín Fánach.

TRANSLATION

No more — no more in Cashel town
    I'll sell my health a-raking,
Nor on days of fairs rove up and down,
    Nor join the merry-making.
There, mounted farmers came in throng
    To try and hire me over,

89

But now I'm hired, and my journey's long,
  The journey of the Rover!

I've found, what rovers often do,
  I trod my health down fairly,
And that wand'ring out on morning's dew
  Will gather fevers early.
No more shall flail swing o'er my head,
  Nor my hand a spade-shaft cover,
But the banner of France float o'er my bed,
  And the *pike* stand by the Rover!

When to Callan, once, with hook in hand,
  I'd go to early shearing,
Or to Dublin town — the news was grand
  That the "Rover gay" was nearing.
And soon with good gold home I'd go,
  And my mother's field dig over —
But no more — no more this land shall know
  My name as the "Merry Rover!"

Five hundred farwells to Fatherland!
  To my loved and lovely Island!
And to Culach's boys — they'd better stand
  Her guards by glen and highland.
But now that I am poor and lone,
  A wanderer — not in clover —
My heart it sinks with bitter moan
  To have ever lived a Rover.

In pleasant Kerry lives a girl,
  A girl whom I love dearly,
Her cheek's a rose, her brow's a pearl,
  And her blue eyes shine so clearly!
Her long fair locks fall curling down
  O'er a breast untouched by lover;
More dear than dames with a hundred poun'
  Is she unto the Rover!

Ah, well I mind when my own men drove
  My cattle in no small way,
With cows, with sheep, with calves they move,
  With steeds, too, west to Galey;
Heaven willed I'd loose each horse and cow,
  And my health but half recover,
But it breaks my heart, for her sake, now
  That I'm only a sorry Rover.

But when once the French come o'er the main,
  With stout camps in each valley,
With Buck O'Grady back again,
  And poor, brave Tadhg O'Dalaigh,

O, the Royal Barracks in dust shall lie,
   The yeoman we'll chase over,
And the English clann be forced to fly,
   'Tis the sole hope of the Rover!

Here are the words of "The Girl I left behind me".
I'm lonesome since I crossed the hills and o'er the moor that's sedgy,
With heavy thoughts my mind is filled since I have parted with Peggy.
Whene'er I turn to view the place, the tears doth fall and blind me,
When I think on the charming grace of the girl I left behind me.

The hours I remember well, when next to see doth move me,
The burning flames my heart doth tell since first she owned she loved me
In search of someone fair and gay several doth remind me,
I know my darling loves me well, though I left her far behind me.

The bees shall lavish, make no store, and the dove become a ranger,
The fallen water cease to roar, before I'll ever change her.
Each mutual promise faithfully made by her whom tears doth blind me,
And bless the hour I pass away with the girl I left behind me.

My mind her image full retains, whether asleep or waking,
I hope to see my jewel again, for her my heart is breaking.
If ever I chance to go that way, and she has not resigned me,
I'll reconcile my mind and stay with the girl I left behind me.

[In *Popular Music of the Olden Time*, Vol.II, p.709, Chappell quotes
from a letter which he received from Bunting in 1840 in which he
says of "The Girl I left behind me":— "It is a pretty tune, and has
been played for the last fifty years, to my knowledge, by the fifes
and drums, and bands of the different regiments, on their leaving
the towns for new quarters."]

58. PLANXTY MISS BURKE

TITLE: *1840, p.43:* Plangsty Miss Burke. Index, p.V: Planxroe inghean Ni
Bhuairchidh. Tune: MS.33, bk.5, p.76: "Plangsty Miss Burke, by Carolan".

NOTES

Noted from Arthur O'Neill, the harper in 1800. (Index p.IX).

No words are extant for this pretty tune, which is typical of Carolan. The Burkes of County Galway were an important family in Carolan's time, but in the absence of the Christian name it is not possible to identify the lady who is the subject.

Also, it is not unlikely that the air was not composed for one of the Burkes. There are earlier versions (all inferior) in Lee's *Collection* (1780), Thompson's *Hibernian Muse* (1786) and Mulholland's *Collection* (1810), in all of which the title is "John Kelly". There were two country gentlemen of this name in Carolan's time, both in the province of Connaught, and both known to Carolan.

[See *DOSC* I, p.203, and II, p.46.]

59. FIGHIM-SE LÍON IS OLANN
I weave linen and wool

TITLE: *1840, p.44:* I can weave linen. Index, p.IV: Fighimse lín is olan. Tune: MS.5, p.80: "I can weave linen and woolen. From J.Mc C."

NOTES

Noted from John McCracken, Belfast in 1800 (Index p.VIII). The published version has an extra four bars marked 'Chorus', but these are not in the MS. version.

92

60. IS GALAR CRÁIDHTE AN GRÁDH
Love's a tormenting pain

TITLE: *1840, p.44:* Love's a tormenting pain. Index, p.IV: Is galar cráite an grádh. Tune: *1840*, p.44.

NOTES
Noted from Denis Hempson at Magilligan in 1796. Bunting states that it was composed in 1670 by William Connellan the harper-composer, whose more celebrated brother was Thomas Connellan.

[In *Stanford – Petrie* No.1573, obtained from Frank Keane, Co. Clare, is a version of Bunting's air entitled "Mo chreach is mo dhith, is claoidhte an galar an gradh" ("Alas and alack, love is a dreadful affliction"). The MS. copy which is almost identical to the *1840* version, is in MS.27, p.62. It is marked "Supposed by Hempson to be one of W. Conlan's tunes and called the Golden Hero (?). From Hempson at Belfast in 1792". See also MS.3, 87 of the *Goodman MSS* ("Is claoite 'n galar an grádh").]

61. LADY BLAYNEY

TITLE: *1840, p.45:* Lady Blayney. By Carolan. Index, p.II: "Bantiaghearna Blanadh". Tune: MS.33, bk.3, p.2 — "Lady Blaney. By Carolan".

NOTES

In the MS. Bunting states that he obtained this air from Rose Mooney, but in the Index of the *1840* volume he gives Charles Fannin as the source. Both were harpers. The piece is not suited to words, and none are extant. [There is a rough notation of the tune in MS. 29, p.39. The time signature, which is given as 2/4 time in both MSS., has been changed to 'alla breve' in the above printed tune by Donal O'Sullivan. See *DOSC* I, p.168 and 2, p.6].

The founder of the Blaney family in Ireland was Edward Blaney of Montgomery. Having served in Spain and the Low countries, he accompanied the Earl of Essex to Ireland in 1598, as a Colonel in the Army. He was present at the siege of Kinsale in 1601 and was made Governor of Mount Norris in the same year. In 1603 he was knighted at Dublin Castle and he became Seneschal of Co. Monaghan in 1604. By patents, in 1607 and 1611, he received large grants of territory in that county and in 1621 was created Lord Blayney, Baron of Monaghan.

The subject of Carolan's air is probably Mary, the wife of the 6th Baron, whom she later married in 1686. She was the daughter of William Caulfield, 1st Earl of Charlemony by Sarah, daughter of Charles Moore Viscount Drogheda. At the date of her marriage she was the widow of Arthur Dillon of Lismullen, Co. Meath.

Lord Blayney succeeded to the title in 1689 and was one of the few Protestants who attended King James's Irish Parliament in that year, according to the list of members. He later fled to England and was consequently attainted, but King William's victory ensured the restoration of his estates. At various times he was Governor of Monaghan and Governor of Sligo, and he took his seat in the Irish House of Lords on the 5th October, 1692. Lord Blayney died on the 3rd January, 1705 and Lady Blayney onthe 8th August 1724. Both are buried in the Chapel of Castle Blaney which he built. The title became extinct on the death unmarried of the 12th Baron in 1874.

62. MOLLY ASTHORE
Molly My Treasure

TITLE: *1840, p.46:* Molly, my treasure. Index, p.IV: Maire a stor — Mary, my treasure. Tune: *1840*, p.46.

NOTES

Noted from Charles Fannin, the harper, in 1792 (Index, p.IX).

The celebrity of this beautiful air is due to the fact that Thomas Moore used it for his famous song "The harp that once through Tara's halls" in the first number of the *Melodies* (1807). Moore took it from Thomson's *Scottish Airs*, set 1 (1793) or, less probably, O'Farrell's *Collection* (c.1797-1800), p.46. The title in both cases is "Gramachree".

As regards the two titles, "asthore" is phonetic for "a stóir", meaning "my store" or "my treasure"; and "gramachree" is phonetic for "grádh mo chroidhe" — "love of my heart".

The earliest printed form of the tune is in William McGibbon's *Scots Tunes*, bk.II (1746) under the title "Will you go to Flanders" (reprinted in Moffat's *Minstrelsy of Ireland*, p.351). The first verse is given in David Herd's *Ancient and Modern Scottish Songs* (1776), Vo.II:

Will you go to Flanders, my Mally O?
Will you go to Flanders, my Mally O?
 There we'll get wine and brandy,
 And sack and sugar candy;
Will you go to Flanders, my Mally O?

The best-known song to the tune is by the Rt. Hon. George Ogle (1742-1814), who represented the City of Dublin in Grattan's Parliament and voted against the Union with Britain. It is printed in *Songs of the Gael*, First Series (1922), compiled by the late Rev. Pádruig Breathnach, pp.30-31. The first verse is as follows:

As down by Banna's banks I strayed
 One evening in May,
The little birds, in blithest notes
 Made vocal every spray.
They sung their little notes of love,

96

They sung them o'er and o'er.
Ah! Grá Machree ma Cholleen Oge,
'Shee Molly veg Masthore!

The last two lines are phonetic Irish for:

Ó! grádh mo chroidhe mo chailín óg,
'Sí Mailí bheag mo stór!
(The young girl is my heart's love, Little Molly is my treasure.)

The Editor of *Songs of the Gael* was given this version of the air by a priest: "He took down the version fifty years ago from the singing of an old woman in County Carlow, who was then nearly a hundred years old. She had learned the version from her grandmother" [An interesting variant of the tune is to be found in Bunting's *1840* volume p.67 entitled "Little Molly O!". (See notes to No.90 in this edition). The tune is also printed on p.17 of the Introduction to the *1840* volume.]

63. TABHAIR DOM DO LÁMH
Give me your hand

TITLE: *1840, p.40:* Give me your hand. Index, p.VI: Tabhar dham do lámh. Tune: MS.27, p.96.

NOTES

[The Index (p.VIII) states that this piece was composed by Rory Dall Ó Cahán in 1603 and was notated from the playing of Arthur O'Neill, the harper in 1806. For a note on Rory Dall see *DOSB* VI, 42. We find in O'Neill's *Memoirs* (MS.46, p.27) the following account: "He [Rory Dall] took a fancy to visit Scotland where there were great harpers. He took his retinue (or suit) with him. Amongs other visits in the style of an Irish chieftain he paid one to a lady Eglinton, and she not knowing his rank in a peremptory manner demanded a tune which he declined, as he only came to play to amuse her, and in an irritable manner left the house. However, when she was informed of his consequence she eagerly contrived a reconciliation and made an apology, and the result was that he composed a tune for her ladyship, the handsome tune of "Da Mihi Manum" (Give me your hand) for which his fame spread thro' Scotland . . . ." The following is a list of references from the edition of Neal's *Celebrated Irish Tunes* by Anne Willis:

Wright's *Aria di Camera*, 36 (1730)
Neal's *Celebrated Irish Tunes*, p.3(b) (c.1726)
Burk Thumoth's *Twelve English and Twelve Irish Airs*, 41 (c.1745-50) Thompson's *Hibernian Muse*, 12 (c.1786).
Brysson's *Curious Selection of Favourite Tunes*, 22b (c.1790)
Mulholland's *Ancient Irish Airs*, 8 (1810).]

64. HUGH O'DONNELL

TITLE: *1840, p.47:* Planxty Hugh O'Donnell. Index, p.V: Planxtae Aodha Mic Domhneil. Tune: MS.29, p.12: "Plangsty O'Donnell". The last four bars are missing and are taken from the 1840 version.

NOTES

The air, which is by Carolan, was noted by Bunting from Charles Byrne the harper in 1792. The air appeared earlier in *Compositions of Carolan*. The subject is one of the sons of Colonel Manus O'Donnell of Newport, Co. Mayo. The Colonel was a great-grandson of Niall Garbh O'Donnell, who was promised the earldom of Tyrconnell both by Elizabeth and by James. Instead he was brought to England in 1608 and languished in the Tower of London until his death twenty years later. Carolan composed pieces for both the father and the son, Hugh. Hugh married Maud Browne, of Mount Browne, Co. Mayo, in 1728. [Two other notations, both more or less similar are in MS 33, bk.3, p.13, and MS 33, bk.5, p.53. See *DOSC* I p.231, and 2, p.78.]

65. THE ROBBER or CHARLEY REILLY

TITLE: *1840, p.48:* The Robber of Charley Reilly. Index, p.II: An Foghlaidhe.
Tune: MS.13, p.100.

WORDS: MS.29

In Newry town I was bred and born,
At St. Stephen's Green I die in scorn.
I served my time to the saddling trade,
I always was a roving blade.

At seventeen I took a wife,
I loved her dear as I loved my life;
And to maintain her fine and gay
A-robbing went on the King's highway.

O when my money it did grow low,
On the King's highway I was forced to go.
I robbed both lords and ladies bright,
Carried home the gold to my heart's delight.

I never robbed no poor man yet,
Nor any tradesman caused I to fret.
I robbed both lords and ladies bright,
Carried home the gold to my heart's delight.

To Covent Garden I took my way,
With my blooming wife for to see the play:
Where Fielding's gang did me pursue,
Taken I was by that cursed crew.

My father cries, "I am undone!"
My mother cries for her darling son.
My wife she tore her golden hair —
"What shall I do? I'm in deep despair."

And when I'm dead and in my grave,
A decent funeral let me have:
Six highwaymen to carry me,
Give them broad swords and sweet liberty.

Six blooming girls to bear my pall,
Give them white gloves and ribbons all.
And when I'm dead they'll tell the truth —
He was a wild and a wicked youth.

NOTES

AIR and WORDS: [Noted at Drogheda in 1803 (Index, p.XI). The tune is a variant of "Cailín ó chois tSiúire" also known as "The Croppy Boy" and a detailed note by Breandán Breathnach is in the Journal *Ceol*, Vol. II, No.IV, pp.94 and 95.

Various versions of the song are to be found in the English folk song collections. A complete list of these occurrences in the 19th and 20th cent. collections is in *A Guide to English Folk Song Collections* (Liverpool 1954) by Margaret Dean-Smith.

One version, in *A Garland of English Folk Songs*, (1926) by F. Kidson, begins as follows: "In Newlyn town I was born and bred." Song No. 326 in *Folksongs of Britain and Ireland* by Peter Kennedy is entitled "Newlyn Town" and is another variant, collected in Suffolk in 1955.]

66. UAIR BHEAG ROIMH A' LÁ
A little hour before day

TITLE:*1840, p.48:* A little hour before day. Index, p.VI: Uair Bheag Roimh Lá. Tune: MS.33, bk.3, p.39.

"A dhochtúir dhílis, túir 'om teagasc,
    Uairín roimh an lá inniubh,
Nó cionnus a dhéanfadh bean óg leanbh
    Uairín roimh an lá inniubh?"

"Cos léi shíneadh agus cos léi chrapadh,
'S a cúl a thabhairt go dlúth dhon leabaidh,
Leabhar a thabhairt ná déanfadh a mhalairt,
Uairín roimh an lá inniubh.''

"A dhochtúir dhílis, túir 'om teagasc,
Uairín roimh an lá inniubh,
Nó cionnus a bhéarfadh bean óg leanbh
Uairín roimh an lá inniubh?''
"Cos léi ar an iarta agus cos léi ar a' dtáirsigh,
Agus liú go h-árd ar mhnáibh a' bhaile,
Agus siúd mar a bhéarfadh bean óg leanbh,
Uairín roimh an lá inniubh.''

" 'S a dhochtúir dhílis, túir 'om teagasc,
Uairín roimh an lá inniubh,
Nó cionnus mar a bhréagfadh bean óg leanbh
Uairín roimh an lá inniubh?''
"Sáspan plúir agus púntán ime,
Agus leabaidh chlúimh i gcúinne na tine,
Agus siúd mar a bhréagfadh bean óg leanbh,
Uairín roimh an lá inniubh.''

TRANSLATION
1. "Doctor dear, please tell me, A little hour before day, How does a young
woman beget a child A little hour before day?" "Stretch one leg and shrink the
other, And lay her back firmly on the bed Give her a stroke, and nothing else,
A little hour before day." 2. "Doctor dear, please tell me, A little hour before
day, How does a young woman bear a child A little hour before day?" "One leg
to the right and one leg to the left, A shout loudly to the woman of the house,
And that is how a young woman bears a child A little hour before day." 3.
"Doctor dear, please tell me, A little hour before day, How does a young woman
soothe a child A little hour before day?" "A saucepan of flour and a bit of
butter, And a feather bed in the chimney-corner, And that is how a young
woman soothes a child A little hour before day."

NOTES
AIR and WORDS: The air (p.48) was noted from Charles Byrne
the harper in 1806. The following single verse in MS.10, No.79 may
also have been contributed by him:

"A dhochtúir dhílis, tabhair dom breathnamh
    Uair bheag a roimhe lá,
Guid é an chaoi a bhfearr 'bhreith leinibh
    Uair bheag a roimhe lá?''
"Druid do ghlúna 'gus dún do ghlaca,
Agus gabh naoi n-uaire tímcheall teallaigh,
Gabh anonn 's gabh anall 'san teach — 'sí an breathnamh,
    Uair bheag a romhe lá.''

"Doctor dear, give me advice, a little hour before day, What is the best way to bear a child, A little hour before day?" "Draw your knees together and clench your fists, And walk nine times round the hearth, Go hither and thither through the house — that's the advice, A little hour before day."

The three verses printed under the tune are from the mansucripts of my friend the late A. Martin Freeman, bk.6, pp.51-52. They were noted by him from Conny Cochlan, of Derrynasagart, West Cork in 1914. Mr. Freeman's notable collection from this district (which was then Irish-speaking) was published in volume VI of the *Journal of the Folk Song Society*, 1922, and the third verse was printed under the tune. Verses 1 and 2 have not been printed before.

The elderly singer commented: "Tá eólas go tréan aige na dochtúirií, ma bíonn skeleton aca agus rudaí eile nach eadh, agus bíonn siad a' fiachaint ortha gach éin lá, agus nuair fhéachan dochtúir ort do chidheann sé díreach mar atá'n tú." Mr. Freeman did not print this but he translated it as follows (*Journal*, VI, pp.273-4): "Doctors know everything; for they have skeletons, and other things besides, and they are looking at them every day; and when a doctor looks at you he sees you exactly as you are."

[See the Goodman MSS. 3.59 for a tune entitled "Uair Bheag Ghoirm Roimh An La."
The F sharp used occasionally in the published version along with the B natural and the C sharp in bar 9 is another one of the many instances throughout the collection where Bunting altered a tune for harmonic reasons. The MS. gives us the tune in its correct aeolian mode.

In *Irish Folk Music* by O'Neill (Chicago 1910) p.70, the author remarks that this air is "unquestionably a version of 'Seán Ó Duibhir an Gleanna'." This is borne out by the version in Roche's *Collection*, Vol. 1, p.16]

In *Stanford-Petrie* there are two tunes more or less related to Bunting's, Nos.1079 and 1080, both entitled "Uair bheag roimh an lá" and a third, No.1472, headed "A dhochtúir dhílis". The title of this last piece in Petrie's MS. is "A dhochtúir dhílis, tabhair dom teagasy" which is a close variant of Bunting's opening line.

[Roche's *Collection of Irish Airs, Marches and Dance Tunes*, Vol. 3, p.5, No.17 has a variant entitled "Uair roimh breachadh an lea or Farewell to Ardmore".]

67. FANNY POWER

TITLE: *1840, p.49:* Fanny Power. Index, p.III: Fannuidh Power. Tune: MS.33, bk.3, p.15.

Is mian liom labhairt ar óig-mhnaoi shuairc,
  Is uaisle geanamhla gnaoi 'gus cáil;
Do bhíos ar a' mbaile tá ar bhruach Loch Riach,
  Táim buidheach gur casadh mé láimh léi.
Nár fhágaidh mé an saoghal go raibh mé go h-acmhuinneach
A' damhsa go h-aerach is mé ar a bainis-se;
Fuagraim an té sin a d'iarrfadh choidh'e spré leat,
  A phéarla linibh na mbán-ghlac.

Siúd í an ainnear ar thaobh a' chuain,
  'S na mílte fear dul a dh'éag dá grádh;
'Sí Fanny is geanamhla na ndlaoi 's na ndual,
  Fuair buaidh ar mhaise 's ar áille.
Is aerach 's is tréitheach an mhaighdean bhreagh sgafanta,
Mian croidh na h-Éireann an péarla deas galanta;
Ólaighid a sláinte 's ná déanaigidh faillighe
  Fá thuairim Fanny nín Dáibhidh.

TRANSLATION

I wish to speak of the gracious girl, Noblest and loveliest in face and character; I was in the village on the shores of Loughrea, I am grateful that I happened to meet her. May I not quit this life until I am energetically Dancing with joy at her wedding; I denounce anyone who would ever ask a dowry with you, Beautiful young lady of the white hands. 2. This is the maiden beside the lake, With men in their thousands dying for love of her; 'Tis Fanny is fairest in tresses and locks, Who excelled in grace and beauty. Pleasant and accomplished is this lovely, spirited girl, The heart's desire of Ireland, the pretty tasteful beauty; Drink her health and do not fail To toast Fanny, the daughter of David.

AIR: Entitled in the MS: "Madame Trench or Fanny Power, by Carolan. From Charles Byrne." But in the Index of *1840* he states that he noted it from Arthur O'Neill. [There is a rough copy in MS. 29, p.22.]

WORDS: Noted from William Bartley by Bunting's amanuensis Patrick Lynch. This piece is included in my edition of Carolan: the air in Vol. I, p.246 and notes in Vol. II, p.97. Fanny Power was the daughter and heiress of David and Elizabeth Power of Coorheen, Loughrea, County Galway. She married, on the 13th March, 1732, Richard Trench of Garbally in the same county. Their eldest son, born in 1741, was created Baron Kilconnel in 1797.

68. MÁIRE ÓG NA gCIABH
Young Mary of the Tresses

TITLE: *1840, p.49:* Mary with the fair locks. Index, p.IV; Máire óg na gciabh.
Tune: MS.33, bk. I, p.32. No key or time signature. Very rough notation.

WORDS: MS.7, No.41.

A Mháire óg na gciabh, cuir do dhóchas i nDia,
Ná h-ísligh is ná h-árdaigh is ná fágaibh mé i bpian,
Nó rachad thar sliabh, mar chomhnuigheas an fiadh,
Imeasc na ngleanntán ag déanamh leanndubh gur leat do chaill mé mo chiall.

Siubhlfaidh mé an tslighe agus na bóithre so síos,
Mar bhfuil an stáid-bhean chiúin mhodhmhar, 'sí thoigfeadh an tuirse so dhíom.

105

Le glór binn a cinn bhéarfadh an rón glas ón dtuinn,
An crón-torc ón gceo-chnoc is an smóilín ón gcoill.

TRANSLATION

1. Young Mary of the tresses, put your trust in God, Do not lower, do not raise, and do not leave me in pain, Or I shall go over the mountain, where the deer abides, Amid the glens, grieving because you have cost me my senses 2. I shall walk the pathway and down these roads, Where lives the quiet, modest, fair girl who will lift this weariness from me. At the sweet sound of her voice the grey seal will come from the waves, The brown boar from the misty hill and the little thrush from the wood.

NOTES

Noted at Deel Castle Ballina, County Mayo, in 1792.

In a note on page 90 of the Introduction, Bunting states that "the words bear internal marks of a very high antiquity". His reason is that "the wild boar has not been seen in Ireland for many hundred years" Actually, it was not extinct in either Ireland or England in the middle of the eighteenth century.

[Another version of the words is to be found in MS.11, p.10.]

69. CATHAL MHAC AODH
Charles Magee

TITLE: *1840, p.50:* Charles Machugh — the wild boy. Index, p.III: Cathal Mhac Aodha. Tune: MS.33, bk.3, p.64.

A fhlaithe Mhic Dé, bheir solus don ngréin,
Go seachnaigh tú mé ar earráid an tsaoghail,
'S nach bhfuil oiread an éin a labhras a bhéal
Nach ndeireann liom féin gur shladaigh mé siubhal.

Thug siad a n-éitheach, ní gadaidhe mé féin,
Ach buachaill beag aerach earráideach baoth,
'S má mheallaim luach éadaigh ó bhodaigh an Bhéarla,
Cia bhiadh 'n-a dhéigh ar Chathail Mhac Aodh?

TRANSLATION

1. Princely Son of God, that brings light to the sun, Put me on my guard against the errors of life, And there's not a single bird that opens his mouth That doesn't say to me that I am a roving robber. 2. They are liars, I am not a robber, But a lively little lad, reckless and prone to error, And if I coax the price of a suit of clothes from the English churls, Who would blame Cathal Magee?

NOTES

The tune was noted from Charles Byrne the harper in 1792. The words are in MS.10, No. 74, origin unstated. Cathal Magee was a famous highwayman in Ulster. There is a version of the words in Lloyd's *Duanaire na Midhe* (1914), pp.74-5: 7 verses, of which verses 3 and 4 correspond to our 1 and 2.

70. SÉAMUS AN CHACA
James the Coward

TITLE: *1840, p.50:* Dirty James. Index, p.V: Séamus a' chaca a chaill Éire — Dirty James that lost Ireland. Tune: MS.33, bk.4, p.42.

NOTES

This tune, for which no words are extant, was noted from Charles Byrne the harper in 1806. The subject is, of course, James II, the last of the Stuart kings; but to state that "he lost Ireland" is misleading. He was the last of his line, and the circumstances in which he was succeeded in 1688-9 by William of Orange and his wife Mary are a matter of history. The theory of divine right of kings was destroyed in England, and a king and queen were set up who owed their position to the choice of parliament. As the English had conquered the Irish, William of Orange became King of Ireland.

The word *chaca* in the title is the genitive of *cac* meaning "excrement", so the English translation is "James of the excrement". As this is somewhat unpleasant, I have chosen the title given in Dinneen's Dictionary: "Séamus an chaca, James the Coward, a name given to King James II of England". At the same time, it seems fair to say that James was not a coward. He left England for France in circumstances that left him no alternative.

[The inclusion of the extra bar at the end of each part in the MS. version may have been Bunting's method of indicating that the first part was to be played between each of the three parts and again at the end of the third part. The published version omits the extra bar. 'Lesley's March' in Oswald's *Caledonian Pocket Companion*, I p.36, may be related to the Bunting tune.]

CHARLES BYRNE

ARTHUR O'NEILL

71. AN SÚISÍN BÁN
The White Blanket

TITLE: *1840, p.51:* The white blanket. Index, p.VI: Suisín Ban. Tune: *1840, p.51.*

WORDS: MS.10, p.139

Cuirim díbirt ar an aoise seo a chaoidhche 's go bráth,
Is craobhsgaoileadh air as taoibh ós fíochmhuil domh a rádh.
Dá bhfuighinn faoidhche naoi n-oidhche le n-aideamhuin mo ghrádh,
Choiscfinn ciocras go faoibhreach faoi an tsúisín bán.

Ins an órd sin 'sé brón domh ná bhfuigheam go bráth
A bheith suidhe i gcóisir na h-óige ná i gcumann le mnáibh.
Sul a dtóirling don mbán-chnoc go mbéidir a rádh
Go bhfuair sí *cóireadh* fá dhó uaim faoi an tsúisín bán.

Ní chuirim cáin ar na mnáibh feasta go bráth ins an oidhche
A bhéaradh fascadh dá mbán-chrios i n-aice le mo chroidhe,
Chuireadh lámh dheas na mbán-bhas tharm 's mé mo luighe,
Is bhéarfadh fáilte agus grádh dhomh faoi an tsúisín buidhe.

111

TRANSLATION

1. I put banishment on this age for ever and aye, And I proclaim it because it makes me furious to say so. If I got a space of nine nights to tell my love, I would cease my desperate yearning underneath the white blanket. 2. In this [religious]Order 'tis my grief that I am never able To attend a party of young people or to enjoy the society of women. Before I come down from the white mountain may I be able to say That I have twice enjoyed an assignation under the white blanket. 3. Henceforth I shall never blame the women at night-time That would press their fair girdle close to my heart, That would stretch the fair palms of their right hands across me as I lay, And that would give love to me and welcome under the yellow blanket.

NOTES

Noted at Deel Castle, Ballina, County Mayo in 1792 (Index, p.XI).

There are several versions of both air and words, under different titles. A complete list is given in *DOSB* Vol.I, p.65, in connection with the song *Casadh an tSúgáin* (The Twisting of the Rope) printed in *Bunting 1796*. The list includes a different air to which the words were sung: A' gcluin tú leat mé, a ghiolla chuaidh a d'iarraidh na mná?, meaning "Listen to me, young man who is looking for a wife". [See also the Goodman MSS.I.11. The fair copy of the tune, as published in the *1840* Volume, is in MSS. 27, p.56.]

Dr. Douglas Hyde includes the song in his *Love Songs of Connacht*, pp.74-76, with an English translation and an explantory note in both languages. The English note has a certain charm because it quaintly follows the Irish:

'Tis the cause of this song — a bard who gave love to a young woman, and he came into the house where she herself was with her mother at the fall of night. The old woman was angry, him to come, and she thought to herself what would be the best way to put him out again, and she began twisting a sugaun [súgán] or straw rope. She held the straw, and she put the bard a-twisting it. The bard was going backwards as the sugan was a-lengthening, until at last he went out on the door and he ever-twisting. When the old woman found him outside she rose up of a leap and struck the door in his face. She then flung his harp out to him through the window, and told him to be going."

72. DO BHÍ BEAN UASAL
There once was a lady

TITLE: *1840, p.52:* There was a young lady. Index, p.III: Do Bí Bean Uasal. Tune: MS.33, bk.I, p.32: "Do bhi Bean Uasal. Bhi mise la gabhail". "The same air to both. D.M." A rough copy.

WORDS: MS.7, No.105

Do bhí bean uasal, seal dá luadh liom,
'S do chuir mé suas dí, faraoir géar!
Agus phós mé cuairsge na mala gruama,
Do rinne gual do mo chroidhe go léir.
Tobac mo thórraimh bíonn ins a' gcófra,
Sin is mo chónra 's a' teach úd thíos;
Mo léan mo bhó-eallach a' tiacht tráthnóna,
Na gamhna leófa 'gus iad a' diúl.

A chailín donn deas ar a dhúbhluigheas m'annsacht,
Ins a' gcontabhairt tabhair dhom póg,
Dá ngluaisfeá liom-sa faoi bhruach na gcoillte
Go Baile na hInnse mar'mbíonn an ceól,
Dá mbeadh mo mhuinntir uile a' cainnt ort,
Cár mhisde liom-sa é, a mhíle stór?
'S gur fris na Gearaltaigh gach aon lá margaidh
A bhíos mo *valentine* is mise ag ól.

Is tinn 's is brónach a bhím Dia Domhnaigh,
'S gan fhios mo dhóláis ag neach dhon saoghal;
'S gur litir fuair mé a sgríobh mo ró-ghrádh
Go raibh mé móran a' dul dhon tslighe.
Is leat-sa shiulfainn go ciúin na bóithre,
Dá dtabhairfeá móide nach mbeitheá claon,
'S dá bhfuighinn-se bás is mo shíneadh i' gcónra,
A Dhé, cia phógfadh í, bláth na gcaor.

TRANSLATION

1. There once was a lady bethrothed to me, And she gave me up, to my bitter grief! And I married a rough woman with frowning brows, Who turned my whole heart to coal. Tobacco for my wake is in the chest, And my coffin, too, is in yonder house; I grieve for my cattle, returning at evening, The calves are with them, and they suckling. 2. Pretty brown-haired girl for whom I have doubled my love, In this hazard give me a kiss. Come with me by the edge of the woods To Ballinahinch where there is always music. If all my people were talking

113

about you, What does that matter to me, my thousand treasures? And it is with the Fitzgeralds on each market-day My sweetheart and I are drinking. 3. Sick and sorrowful am I every Sunday, With not a soul knowing my grief; 'Tis that I got a letter written by my beloved That I was going far astray. 'Tis with you I would walk the roads in peace, If you would swear that you would not be false to me. And if I should die and be lying in a coffin, My God! who would kiss her, the flower of the rowan berry?

NOTES
[Noted from "R. Stanton, Westport, in 1802". The words are also to be found on a loose sheet in MS.26. Another copy in MS.25, p.100 has the note: "From Redmond Stanton, a blind man at Westport." Verse 1 of the above words appears as Verse VII of a poem attributed in some MS. to Cathal Buí Mac Giolla Gunna in Breandán O Buachall's book, *Cathal Buí.*]

73. MISS FETHERSTON or CAROLAN'S DEVOTION

TITLE: *1840, p.53:* Carolan's Devotion. Index, p.II: Brabhadh Cearbhallain. Tune: Neale's *Celebrated Irish Tunes*, p.22. See my edition of Carolan, Vol. I, p.190 and Vol. II, pp.30-31.

On a fair Sunday morning devoted to be
Attentive to a sermon that was ordered for me,
I met a fresh rose on the road by decree,
And though Mass was my notion, my devotion was she.
 Welcome, fair lily, white and red,
 Welcome was every word we said:
Welcome, bright angel of noble degree,
I wish you would love, and that I were with thee.
I pray don't frown at me with mouth or with eye —
So I told the fair maiden, with heart full of glee,
Though the Mass was my notion, my devotion was she.

NOTES

[A similar version of this air is to be found in MS.33, bk.2, p.25, and it is this tune that is the source of Bunting's printed version.]

The circumstances in which this song was composed are recounted by Walker in his *Irish Bards* on the authority of Charles O'Connor. A Miss Fetherston, of County Longford, was on her way to church service in Grandard when she met Carolan, who apparently was going to Mass. She introduces herself and Carolan replies that he has heard of her as "a young lady of great beauty and much wit". She tells him that she has long been charmed by his musical compositions and invites him to visit her house. He promises to do so, and later, at Mass, "instead of praying for Miss Fetherston, as she requested, he neglected his religious duties to compose a song on her".

In his *Irish Minstrelsy* (1831), p.liv, Hardiman gives the verse printed above, and no more have been found. It was the only occasion on which Carolan composed words in English, and Hardiman explains that "this was an act of poetic gallantry, as the young lady did not understand Irish".

Walker states that the date of the meeting between Carolan and Miss Fetherston (and therefore of the composition of the song) was "either 1720 or 1721", and this is probably correct. Bunting gives two different dates. At the head of the tune (p.53) he has "Composed about 1700", but in the Index (p.VIII) he gives the year as 1690.

It seems probable that the subject of the song was a sister of Thomas Fetherston of Ardagh, near Edgeworthstown, County Longford, who married a Miss Sherlock about 1709.

On one occasion when young Oliver Goldsmith was in the village of Ardagh he inquired for the local inn and was directed by a practical joker to Squire Fetherson's house, the Squire at that time being probably a brother or nephew of Carolan's Miss Fetherston. Goldsmith behaved as if he were at an inn, ordered dinner, and courteously invited the Squire and his daughter to sit at table with him. It was this incident that suggested the plot of *She Stoops to Conquer*.

74. TARRAING GO CAOIN AN SGEÓL
Consider the story well

TITLE: *1840, p.54:* Consider the story. Index, p.VI: Tarraing go caoin an sgeúl.
Tune: MS.33, bk.2, p.81.

Féach-sa Samson ar stríoc,
Á leagadh sa' mbruighion na Philistín,
Tré leigint a chumann le mnaoi
Gurab' aindeiseach críoch a d'imthigh air.

CHORUS: Is tarraing go caoin an sgeól,
Is, a chara bí 'nglóir a' tseanachais:
Má's measa do shlighe ná t-eólas,
Seachain go deó na calaoise.

Féach-sa Hercules líomtha,
Leanbh ba dhruidh bhí ag Jupiter;

116

Tré leigint a chumann le mnaoi
Do rinne súd spríos mór theine dhe.

Is oth liomsa duine dhed' cháil
Tuitim i lár na h-aindeise,
Síor-dhéanamh gliogair le mnáibh,
Is Solamh mhac Dáibh gur, mhealladar.
Tá leagan ar chathair na Traoi,
Mar cailleadh na mílte curadh ann,
Tré Helen gheanamhail mhodamhail
Gur baineadh dá bonn 's gur briseadh iad.

TRANSLATION

1. Consider how Samson fell, Laid low in the fort of the Phillistines Through giving his love to a woman, So that he came to a distressful end. CHORUS: Consider the story well, And, friend, list to the voice of antiquity If your behaviour is worse than your knowledge, Shun those trickeries for ever. 2. Look at outstanding Hercules, A child begotten by Jupiter; Through giving his love to a woman She made a great fire of him. 3. I am troubled that a person of your type Should fall in the midst of misfortune Always prattling with women, And they allured Solomon son of David. 4. There is a legend about the city of Troy, That thousands of warriors fell there Through beautiful, gracious Helen, That were captured on her account and killed.

NOTES

AIR: Noted at Tipperary in 1797. No further particulars are given. [This air is a variant of "Plancam Peirbhig" in *Poets and Poetry of Munster*, Vol.I, pp.92/93. In Flood's *History of Irish Music*, p.248 et seq., the following reference is found:— "A fairly good version of this air was published by Playford in 1713 and by B. Cooke in 1795. (This fine Irish melody was popular in England as 'The Bunter's Delight')".]

WORDS: Bunting MS.7, No.48. Source not stated.

75. CAROLAN'S RECEIPT

TITLE: *1840, p.54:* Carolan's Receipt — or Stafford's Receipt for Whiskey. Index, p.V: Receipt of Chearbhallain. Tune: My edition of Carolan, Vol. I, p.249.

WORDS: Hardiman's *Irish Minstrelsy*, Vol. I, p.22

Má's tinn nó slán do thárlaidheas féin,
Ghluaiseas tráth 's dob fhearrde mé,
Ar cuairt chum Seóin chum sócamhaill d'fhagáil,
An Stafardach breágh sásta nach gnáth gan chéill.
Is i dtaca an mheódhain oidhche do bhíodh sinn ag ól,
Agus ar maidin arís an córdial:
'Sé mheas sé ó mhéainn mhaith gurb é súd an gléas
Le Cearbhallán caoch do bheódhughadh!

CHORUS:
    Seal ar misge, seal ar buile,
    Réabadh téad 's ag dul ar mire,
  An faisiun sin do chleachamar ní sgarfam leis go deo!
    Deirim arís é,
    Is innsim don dtír é,
  Má's maith libh do bheith saoighlach bídh choidhche ag ól!

TRANSLATION
If sick or strong I chanced to be,
I went along — 'twas well for me! —

118

To Doctor John to find relief.
Brave Stafford, skilful leech is he!
About the witching hour we would start our carouse,
By morn our zest for whiskey was the sharper:
Sensible man! for such was his plan
To put life in the poor blind harper!

CHORUS: Sometimes tipsy, sometimes raking,
Wild in frenzy, harpstrings breaking,
The custom that we followed, we will never let it die!
I tell you once again, Sirs,
I always will maintain, Sirs.
For a long and merry life of it, be drinking for aye!

NOTES
The subject of this song was Dr. John Stafford of Elphin, County
Roscommon. He was a life-long friend of Carolan, attended him in
his last illness, and was one of the coffin-bearers at his funeral.
A detailed account of him is given in my edition of *Carolan*, Vol.II,
pp.101-104. In the Index we find that Bunting noted the tune from
Daniel Black in 1796. His version is in the MS.33, bk.2, pp.89-90.
The tune printed above is composite, being the result of a collection
of the following three versions:
  Lee's *Favourite Collection* (1780), p.28
  Walker's *Historical Memoirs of the Irish Bards* (1786), p.15
  Thompson's *Hibernian Muse* (1786), p.2.
The result is a version more suited to the words than any individual
copy of the tune.

76. SWEET PORTAFERRY

TITLE: *1840, p.55:* Sweet Portaferry. Index: p.III: Cuan Milis an Challaidh.
Tune: MS.13, p.107.

[Noted from "J. McCracken Esq. Belfast, 1800." This tune is a variant of No.7 in the *1840* collection, "An londubh agus an chéirseach".]

77. AN BONNÁN BUIDHE
The Yellow Bittern

TITLE: *1840, p.56:* The Yellow Bittern. Index: p.II: Bunnán Buidhe. Tune: Joyce, *Old Irish Folk Music and Songs*, p.314, "From Forde MSS".

NOTES

The air was noted from a "blind man at Westport in 1802" (Index p. XI). There is no MS. copy and the tune given here is from the Forde MS. [The song is still sung today though the Forde version is a closer variant of the present day version than the tune printed by Bunting. It was written by the 18th century Ulster poet, Cathal Buí Mac Giolla Ghunna and two edited versions of the words, including another version of the tune, are to be found in *Cathal Buí* by Breandán Ó Buachalla (Dublin, 1975). The words occur in the Bunting MSS three times: MS. 7, No.73: MS.18, p.35 and MS. 11, p.39. Donal O'Sullivan edited the song in the *Journal of the Irish Folk Song Society*, Vol.20, p.46 and Seán Ó Baoighill published a version in *Cnuasacht de Cheoltaí Uladh.*]

78. MAIDIN BHEAG AOIBHINN
Pleasant Early Morning

TITLE: *1840, p.57:* Soft mild morning. Index, p.IV: Maidin bhog aoibhin. Tune: MS.33, bk.2, p.16.

WORDS: MS.10, No.76

Mo bhrón is mo mhilleadh gan píopa tabac agam,
  Ar a' gleann chaoirthainn d'éirigh an lá,
Agus cailín a' tighe-se bheith sínte ar leabaidh liom,
  Is ar a' gleann chaoirthainn d'éirigh an lá.

Maidin bheag aoibhinn, aoibhinn, aoibhinn,
  Maidin bheag aoibhinn uair roimhe lá,
Is maighdean bheag aoibhinn a' codladh go caoimh liom,
  Is ar a' gleann chaoirthainn d'éirigh an lá.

TRANSLATION
1. Alas and alack that I haven't got a pipe of tobacco, On Glen Kieran it is day-break, And the girl of the house is lying in bed with me And on Glen Kieran it is daybreak. 2. Pleasant, pleasant, pleasant early morning, Pleasant early morning an hour before day, And a lovely little lass sleeping gently with me, And on Glen Kieran it is daybreak.

NOTES
AIR: Noted from Hempson the harper at Magilligan in 1796.

[In MS.33, Bunting writes: — "This seems to be the end rather than the beginning of a tune. From Charles Byrne and poor old Denis Hempson." In the published version, Bunting extends the tune to twice its length by adding sixteen bars not present in the MS. These sixteen bars are a variant of the third section of No.100 in the *1840* collection, "I am asleep and don't waken me". This third section is not in the MS. version.]

79. AN SÚISÍN BUIDHE
The Yellow Blanket

TITLE: *1840, p.58:* The Yellow blanket. Index, p.VI: Suisin Buidhe. Tune: MS.5, p.68.

NOTES

Noted from "P.Quin, Harper, 1806" (Index, p.XI). From the point of view of the words, "Casadh an tSúgáin" and "An Súisín Bán" — sometimes known as "An Súisín Buidhe" — must be accounted as one, for these two songs, if ever they were distinct, have long ago become inextricably intertwined, by reason of identity of meter and similarity of subject, so that it is almost impossible to say, in the case of any particular verse, whether it belongs to one song or the other.

[See also the notes to No.71 in this edition and No.19 (p.65) of Part I of *DOSB*.]

80. O'DONNELL'S MARCH

TITLE: *1840, p.58:* O'Donnell's March. Index, p.IV: Mairseál Ní Dhomhnaill. Tune: MS.33, bk.5, p.52 "O'Donells March".

NOTES

This air was obtained from Richard Stanton, Westport, in 1803.
There is a different air with the same name in the *Feis Ceoil Collection* (1914), p.6.

81. AN CAOINE
The Lament

TITLE: *1840, p.59:* Irish cry, as sung in Ulster. The Goll. The Little Lamentation. Second Goll and Half Chorus. The Great Lamentation. Half Chorus of Sighs and Tears. Index: p.I: An Caoine, gul, caoine bheag, caoine mór; Irish cry, lamentation, little cry, great cry. Tune: MS.5, pp.72/73: No time signature. Rough sketches. Irregular rhythm.

NOTES

[The Index p.VIII gives the source as "O'Neill, harper and from the hired mourners or keeners at Armagh; and from a MS. above 100 years old".

In a note in the Intro. p.88 Bunting indicates that the 'Goll' was "chanted by a single voice". There is another version of this piece on p.2 of the music supplement in the *1840* Introduction. It appears from Bunting's note (p.88) that this version was notated from "professed Keeners in the County of Armagh". The version on p.59 of the *1840* Volume was probably notated from Arthur O'Neill, the harper. In a further reference in the preface (p.7), Bunting mentions the music as "being neither perfect recitative nor perfect melody, but a peculiar combination of both".

The version in MS.5, pp.72/73 does not include the 'Goll' and neither is it divided into sections as in 1840, p.59. With the exception of the 'Goll' section all three versions have one factor in common: — the music moves in various sequential patterns from a high tonic to the tonic an octave below. The version in *1840*, p.59 is the longest and includes a final section where a third theme is introduced and repeated an octave lower. MS.5, pp.72/73 also includes a Leinster Irish cry. From old MSS". and an "Irish cry. Munster. From old MSS".]

82. AN DÉIRCTHEOIR
The Beggar

TITLE: *1840, p.63:* The Beggarman. Index, p.I: An deirctheoir. Tune: MS.13, p.100.

NOTES

This tune was obtained from Dr. George Petrie in 1839. [In MS. 12, (2) there are very rough sketches of the tune.

"The Beggarman's Song", No.26 in Colm Ó Lochlainn's *More Irish Street Ballads* (1965) is a variant of Bunting's tune. The words are also given with the music.

In *Garland of Country Song* London, 1895, the author Baring-Gould remarks that this song is known throughout England, Scotland and Ireland, and that in Scotland the "Beggar" is identified with James V. Original English words are to be found in *The Forsaken Lover's Garland*, and original Scots in *The Scots Musical Museum*. (See *A Guide to English Folk Song Collections* [Liverpool, 1954 by Margaret Dean-Smith).]

83. BEANN AN FHIR RUAIDH
The Red-haired Man's Wife

TITLE: *1840, p.63:* The Caves of Cong. Index: p.VI: Umhaidhe Chonga, nó Bean an Fhir Ruaidh — The Caves of Cong, or Red Man's wife. Tune: MS.33, bk.4, p.17.

WORDS: MS.7, No.83

Tráth théighim-se thart síos bím i príosún ceangailte cruaidh,
Bíonn bóltaigh ar mo chaolaibh 's na mílte glas as sin suas.
D'éireóchainn in áirde mar d'éireóchadh an eala dhon gcuan,
Go sínfinn mo thaobh dheas síos le bean an fhir ruaidh.

Ní dá eallach ná maoin ariamh do thug mise spéis,
Nó do nídh ar a' tsaoighal a chlaoidhead a h-aigne ná a méin.
Mór-chiste an righ is bíodh go dtiobhrainn é uaim,
Ar chúntas faill' oidhche bheith sínte le bean an fhir ruaidh.

A chailín bheag lághach a bhfuil deallra deas in do ghruaidhe,
'Sé an buachaillín bán a b'fhearr liom leat-sa dhá luadh,
Gan fhios age cách dá ndéanfá go bhfuilim faoi ghruaim —
Dá aindeóin chrích Fáil 'sí mo grádh-sa bean an fhir ruaidh.

A bhláth gheal na sgéimh, cuirim céad beannacht leat go lá an luain,
'S go bhfuil mé i dtrap ag an éag le méad is tá tathaigh sí uaim;
'S dá mba eól dhuit-se leigheas, chuirfinn i gcéill dhuit-se m'anacair cruaidh,
'S go síntear mé i gcré sí mo chéad-shearc bean an fhir ruaidh.

TRANSLATION

1. When I go down yonder I am fast-bound in gaol, With bolts on my ankles and a thousand fetters from that up. I would rise high as the swan would rise from the bay, So that I might lay my right side down beside the red-haired man's wife. 2. 'Twas not to her cattle or wealth I ever gave heed, Nor to anything on earth that would affront her mind or her desire. If I had the great treasure of the king I would part with it, On condition that I would have a chance to lie for a night beside the red-haired man's wife. 3. Charming little girl with the lovely radiant cheeks, 'Tis the fair-haired boy I would best like to be engaged to you. With nobody knowing . . . (?) that I am distressed — And in spite of all Ireland my beloved is the red-haired man's wife. 4. Bright blossom of beauty, I send a hundred blessings to you till doomsday, And I am in the grip of death through the way she has treated me (?); If you should know of a cure, I would convey to you my deep distress, And till I am laid in the grave my dearest love is the red-haired man's wife.

NOTES

Obtained from George Petrie in 1839.

Cong is in the County of Mayo, close to the shores of Loch Corrib, in County Galway. I know of no verses associated with it but both words and tune of "Bean an Fhir Ruaidh" are well known. Bunting's set, from MS.7, No.83 is given above.

Neither of the two versions of the tune in Stanford Petrie (Nos. 115 and 1140) are the same as Bunting's published version.

[O'Daly in *Poets and Poetry of Munster* (1860), p.12, gives

127

another version under the title "Loch Léin".

The tune also occurs in MS.33, bk.5, No.78. The MS. copy on which the *1840* version is based as in MS.27 on some extra pages at the end.

An edition of the words, attributed to Cathal Buí Mac Ghiolla Gunna and also to Riocard Bairéad, is to be found in *Cathal Buí* by Breandán Ó Buachalla (Dublin, 1975) under the title "Thíos ag Béal Bearnais".]

84. SLÁINTE ÓN gCUPÁN

TITLE: *1840, p.64:* Health from the cup. Index p.V: Slainte an chupan. Tune: MS.33, bk.3, p.63.

NOTES

[In the Intro. p.96, Bunting writes:— "A pleasing memorial of the celebrated Richard Kirwan of Cregg, by whom it was presented to the editor in 1792. The quaintness and brevity of the air and the fact of its consisting of only one part, are strong arguments of a high degree of antiquity."

The tune is pentachordal with the 6th and 7th notes missing.

This piece is also in Bunting's *1809* volume (p.47) and can be found in *DOSB* V, p.103.]

85. PÁIDÍN Ó RAIFEARTA
Paudeen O'Rafferty

TITLE: *1840, p.64:* Paddy O'Rafferty. Index, p.V: Paidin O'Raibheartaigh. Tune: MS.33, bk.2, p.41, — "Phaidhin a Raverty. This is a capital set. From Mac Cauley of Ballymoney — since dead."

Tá bríste gan bhásta aige Páidín Ó Raifearta,
Casóg gan chába aige Páidín Ó Raifearta,
Tá lán a' tighe páistí aige Páidín Ó Raifearta,
Is d'éaluigh Peig bhán le Páidín Ó Raifearta.

Curfá
Páidín is Páidín is Páidín Ó Raifearta,
Páidín is Páidín is Páidín Ó Raifearta,
Páidín is Páidín is Páidín Ó Raifearta,
Is d'éaluigh Peig bhán le Páidín Ó Raifearta.

Nuair a bhím-se sa' tsráid is tnáite 's lag a bhím,
A' féachaint ins na h-áird i ndiaidh Pháidín Uí Raifearta,
Táim-se gan sláinte 's níl faíl ar mo mhaitheasa,
Ó d'éaluigh Peig bhán le Páidín Ó Raifearta.

129

TRANSLATION

1. Breeches without waist-band has Paudeen O'Rafferty, Coat without collar has Paudeen O'Rafferty, A houseful of children has Paudeen O'Rafferty, And fair Peggy eloped with Paudeen O'Rafferty. Chorus: Paudeen and Paudeen and Paudeen O'Rafferty, Paudeen and Paudeen and Paudeen O'Rafferty, Paudeen and Paudeen and Paudeen O'Rafferty, And fair Peggy eloped with Paudeen O'Rafferty. When I'm on the street it's worried and weak I am; Searching the heights for Paudeen O'Rafferty, Healthless I am and I've lost all prosperity Since fair Peggy eloped with Paudeen O'Rafferty. When I'm on the street it's worried and weak I am, Searching the heights for Paudeen O'Rafferty, Healthless I am and I've lost all prosperity Since fair Peggy eloped with Paudeen O'Rafferty.

NOTES

AIR: From J. McCalley at Ballymoney, Co. Antrim, in 1795. There are versions in O'Farrell's *Pocket Companion for the Irish Pipes,* Vol. I, p.106; Holden's *Collection of Irish Slow and Quick Tunes,* bk.2, p.32: [Brysson's *Curious Selection of Favourite Tunes,* p.11; O'Neill's *Dance Music of Ireland* (No.178); McFadden's *Scotch, English, Irish and Foreign Airs,* Vol.III, No.475, and Murphy's *Irish Airs and Jigs,* p.9.]

WORDS: Page 18 of Part II (1924) of *Cosa Buidhe Árda,* a book-let of songs in the Irish language compiled by the late Fionán Mac Coluim. I have not come across any other version.

86. DERMOT AND HIS LASS

TITLE: *1840, p.65:* Dermot and his lass. Index, p.III: Diarmuid agus a chailín. Tune: See *Notes* below.

One Sunday after Mass
Dermot and his lass
To the green wood did pass,
   All alone, all alone, all alone.
He asked for one pogue,
She called him a rogue,
And struck him with her brogue,
   Oh hone, oh hone, oh hone!

Said he, "My dear joy,
Why will you be coy?
Let us play, let us toy,
   All alone, all alone, all alone."
"If I were too mild,
You are so very wild,
You would get me with child,
   Oh hone, oh hone, oh hone!"

He bribed her with sloes,
And bribed her with nuts,
Then a thorn pricked her foot,
   Halla lu, halla lu, hall lu.
"Let me pull it out."
"You'll hurt me, I doubt,
And make me to shout
   Halla lu, halla lu, halla lu!"

NOTES

The above air and words were first published in Durfey's *Pills to Purge Melancholy*, Vol.IV (1719), p.278. The piece is headed "An Irish Song. Set by Mr. Leveridge". In his 1855 volume, pp.112-113 Petrie printed a different tune, with the first verse of the words. I have reproduced Durfrey's air rather than Bunting's because it is much older and seems more suited to the words. Bunting was given his version by his friend Henry Joy of Belfast in 1800. [It is to be found in MS.5, p.42, and it is virtually identical to the *1840* tune.] As to the Irish words spelt phonetically: *pogue* is *póg*, a kiss: *brogue* is *bróg*, a shoe; *oh hone* is *ochón*, alas; and *halla lu* is *aillilliú*, which has much the same meaning.

87. NÍ MIAN LIOM
I do not intend

TITLE: *1840, p.65:* I do not incline. Index, p.V: Ní mian liom. Tune: MS.5, p.81, "I do not incline. From J. McC."

NOTES
Contributed by J. McCracken, Esq., Belfast, in 1810. The title is presumably the opening of a song in Irish, which I have not traced.

88. CAITLÍN NÍ CHUINN
Kathleen Quinn

TITLE: *1840, p.66:* Kitty Quin. Index, p.III: Caitlín Ní Chuin. Tune: MS.33, bk.2, p.20: "From . . . at Mrs. Burkes, Mount Nephin."

NOTES

I have not traced the title elsewhere, nor any other version of the tune. [Index p.IX states that this piece was collected from Charles Byrne the harper in 1802. There are some similarirites between this tune and No.4, "Huis the Cat", in the same collection.]

89. AN CAILÍN DEAS RUA

TITLE: *1840, p.66:* The pretty red girl. Index, p.III: Cailín deas ruadh. Tune: MS.5, p.52.

NOTES

[In the Index p.IX we find this note:— "Thomas Broadwood Esq. collected in Munster 1815." In the MS. we find "From Thos. B. by Mary McC." In Joyce's *Old Irish Folk Music and Song* (1909) p. 53/54 there is a variant under the same title. He gives the following note:— "I give this fine air as I learned it from a singer in the early days, but an instrumental version, much ornamented will be found in *Bunting 1840* p.66. It is there given in the major but I always heard it sung in the minor. There was an Irish song to it of which I remember the first verse" —

"A bhean a' tighe séimh cuir a déirc amach cun a dóill

Beidh mo phaidir chun Dé a cur Séan agus Rathair do chlóin."

In the *Freeman Collection (Journal of the Folk Song Society*, Vol. VI, No.10) there is another variant under the title "An Bata Druin (The Blackthorn Stick)".

There is a song with a similar title "An Cana Droighean Eille (The Blackthorn cane with a thong)" in Petrie's *Ancient Music of Ireland* (1855), p.36/37. It has the same structure as the Bunting, Joyce and Freeman tunes but is otherwise unrelated.

In O'Neill's *The Music of Ireland* (1903), p.80, the jig tune "The Blackthorn Stick" is unrelated to any of the above tunes.]

90. MOLLY BHEAG Ó!
Little Molly O!

TITLE: *1840, p.67:* Little Molly O. Index, p.IV: Máire Bheag O! Tune: MS.28, p.4: "Old Way of Molly Astore".

NOTES

Noted from Charles Fannin, the harper in 1792. [In the Intro. p.97, Bunting writes: " 'Little Molly' — The undoubted original of "Molly Astore" which however prized as a national air, must be admitted to be no more than an arrangement of this more ancient and not less characteristic melody."

Although Bunting is correct in pointing out the connection between the tune and Molly Astore (No.62 in this edition) there seems to be justification for his statement that the former predates the latter. Both versions were collected from Charles Fannin in 1792. An examination of both versions shows that the form remains the same, A B A¹ B¹, while the meter has changed from double to triple time. In MS.28, p.80, there are very rough sketches of the tune with the note: "Molly Bheag Ó! Original name of Molly astore."

MacBean's *Songs and Hymns of the Gael* (Stirling, 1900), p.9, No.7 contains a version of Bunting's tune in 4/4 time with the title "Mo Mhali Bheag Óg (My Dear Little May)". There are also five verses with the note: "Composed by a Highland officer, who accidentally killed a lady."

The phenomenon of tune variants in different meters is not uncommon in Irish traditional music, one of the most frequent examples of this relationship being found between double jigs and reels, i.e. between 6/8 and ₵ time.]

91. SAINT PATRICK'S DAY

TITLE: *1840, p.67:* Patrick's Day. Index, p.IV: Lá Fhéile Páidric. Tune: MS.6, No.39, "Patrick's Day".

NOTES

[Noted from Patrick Quinn the harper in 1792. Close variants of this tune are also to be found in the following collections:

Thompson's *Hibernian Muse*, p.32

MacFadyen's *Selection of Scotch, English, Irish and Foreign Airs*, Vol. I, No.50

Aird's *A Selection of Scotch, English, Irish and Foreign airs*, Vol. II, No.18

Crosby's *Irish Music Repository*, p.41. "Sheelaghs Wedding" to the air of "St. Patrick's Day in the Morning"

Walker's *Irish Bards*, p.33

O'Neill's *Dance Music of Ireland*, No.975

The following tunes have no connection with the above:

Stanford Petrie, No.1303 "Lá Fhéil Phádraig"

Journal of the Folk Song Society, No.35. "Lá le Pádraig"

Also in *Folksongs Sung in Ulster* by Robin Morton, (Cork, 1970) p.8, No.5, is a song entitled "On Patrick's day in the Morning" collected from Arthur Whiteside, "an 84 year old Northener". There is no connection, however, between this tune and Bunting's tune. See also the Goodman MS.1.2 (Lá le Pádraig).]

92. IS IASCAIRE AR LOCH CEARA MÉ

A variant of this tune is in Bunting's *1809* volume, p.48, entitled "Si casgaire (sic) ar loch — The Fisherman", and is dealt with in *DOSB* V, pp.113 *et seq.*

93. MRS. MAXWELL

TITLE: *1840, p.68:* Madam Maxwell. Index, p.II: Baintighearna Macsbhell.
Tune: MS.33, bk.3, p.52.

[The tune in MS.29 p.98 is the one on which the printed copy is
based and was noted from Charles Fannin the harper in 1792. The
version in MS.33, bk.3, p.52 was noted from Hugh Higgins and is
printed above. The tune is dealt with in *DOSC* I p.217 and *DOSC*
II p.63 and 64.]

The subject of this graceful air is probably Judith, daughter and
heiress of James Barry, of Newtown Barry, Co. Wexford, who was
baptized on the 15th December, 1699 and married John Maxwell
of Farnham, Co. Cavan in June, 1719. Her husband was the son
and heir of the Rev. Henry Maxwell, rector of Derrynoose, Co.
Armagh. He was M.P. for Cavan from 1727 to 1756 and High Sheriff
of that county in 1739. Having succeeded in 1737 to the estate of
Farnham by the death of his cousin the Rev. Robert Maxwell,
he was created 6th May, 1756 Baron Farnham of Farnham, Co.
Cavan. Mrs. Maxwell (by that time Lady Farnham) died on the 5th

April, 1771 in Henrietta Street, Dublin and is buried in Christ Church. No words have been found.

94. 'SÉ MO CHREACH MHAIDNE
Woe is me

TITLE: *1840, p.69*: 'Tis a pity I don't see my love. Index: p.VI: Truagh nach bfaicim mo gradh. Tune: MS.33, bk.3, p.53: "Is truan nogh feckan mo gradh. I do not see my love coming in a boat. I'm sorry I do not see my love. From B.B. From the County Mayo."

'Sé mo chreach mhaidne 's mo chrádh
   Ná feicim mo ghrádh-sa a' tíocht
Aníos faoi mhullach an Mháma
   Nó malaidh an Chnuic Bháin aniar.
Tá mo chroidhe dá shlad i mo lár,
   'S is faide liom lá ná bliain;
'S a chumainn, mur dtagair gan spás,
   Beidh mise faoi chlár i do dhiaidh.

Tarraidh, má thagair, go lá,
   A theachtaire is fearr sa' tír;
Tabhair scéala chugam ón bplanda,
   An dtiocfaidh san áit a mbím.

Uirthi ní rachaidh a n-aimhreas
  Mur duine gan nádúr í;
'S má d'imir sí cluiche an chomhradaigh,
  Beannacht go brách léi bíodh!

TRANSLATION

1. Woe is me, and my distress, That I do not see my love coming Up towards the height of Maam Or by the brow of Knockbawn from the west. The heart in my breast is tormented, And the day seems longer than a year; My beloved, if you do not come at once, I shall be in my coffin for lack of you. 2. If you come, stay till daylight, The finest messenger in the land; Bring me news of the plant Whether she will come to the place I live. I will not distrust her Unless she is a person without feeling; And if she played the "engagement" trick, Good-bye to her for ever!

NOTES

AIR: The Index of *1840* states that it was obtained from Mrs. Fitzgerald at Westport, County Mayo, in 1802. [In the MS. version there are three incomplete bars at the end of the tune marked "Ad libitum".]

WORDS: MS. 7, No.173. It seems probable that Mrs. Fitzgerald is the source. I have not come across any version of either air or words.

95. I WISH I WAS A LITTLE SWALLOW

TITLE: *1840, p.70:* The Little Swallow. Index p.I: Aileog Bheag. Tune: MS.33, bk. 5, p.19: "I wish I was a little Swallow".

NOTES

[Collected at Ballynascreen, Co. Derry in 1803. In the Introduction p.96, Bunting writes:— "Another charming air from Ballynascreen. The words which have been handed down by tradition are simple and appropriate to the air, commencing:—

    I would I were a little swallow,
    I would rise into the air and fly,
    Away to that inconstant rover,
      etc, etc."

In the *1840* volume Bunting repeats the second section of the tune. On p.32 of the Introduction he defines 'Crónán' as "the bass in music", while on p.88, he defines it as "a chorus", which it probably is in the case of the above tune.]

96. RAMBLING BOY

TITLE: *1840, p.71:* I am a poor Rambling Boy. Index, p.IV: Is buachaill goidhaisteach mé. Tune: MS.33, bk.2, p.54: "Rambling Boy from Charles Byrne. This tune affords no proof of great antiquity".

[The Index p.VIII gives the source as "W. Sloane, Esq., Belfast 1799" and states "Very ancient, author and date unknown". The MS. gives the source as Charles Byrne, the harper. In the case of the MS. version above, the inclusion of G sharp in the signature would make the air more credible. If the accidentals on D and B are removed as well, then the tune falls into the aeolian mode. The removal of the accidental on F in the printed version also places it in the aeolian mode.]

97. CAILTLÍN NÍ UALLACHÁIN

TITLE: *1840, p.71:* Kitty Nowlan. Index p.III: Cáit Ní Nualain. Tune: MS.33, bk.3, p.31: "Catalin Ni Dhulacan or Catty Nowlan. Very ancient. From Charles Byrne, Co. Leitrim".

NOTES

[The Index p.IX gives the source as "Byrne, harper, 1806". In Petrie's *Music of Ireland* (1892), p.8 et seq., two variants of the tune are published along with six verses, translations and detailed notes on the song.]

141

98. THE BLACKBIRD

TITLE: *1840, p.72:* The Blackbird. Index p.II: An Londubh. Tune: *Irish Folk Song Journal:* Vol. XX, No.24.

NOTES

[The Index p.X gives the source as "D. O'Donnell, harper, Co. Mayo, 1803". In the Introduction p.92, Bunting writes:— "A very fine air used as a vehicle for Jacobite words (of which the following verse is a specimen) during the war of 1688-90. The air itself bears evident marks of a much higher antiquity.

Once in fair England my blackbird did flourish

He was the chief flower that in it did spring; etc."

The tune, which is still well known today as a set-dance, can also be found in:

Joyce's *Old Irish Folk Music and Songs*, pp.181/182 with an interesting note.

Stanford-Petrie, Nos. 292, 519, 672 and 1379.

O'Neill's *Music of Ireland*, Nos. 199, 200, 201 — three versions.

O'Neill's *Dance Music of Ireland*, No.985.

Journal of the Irish Folk Song Society, Vo.XVIII and Vol.V p.14 — the remainder of the verse given by Bunting is in the same journal Vol. XX, No.23.

O'Farrell's *Pocket Companion*, Vol. II, p.132.

O'Neill's *Irish Minstrels and Musicians*, p.131.

In *Songs of Irish Rebellion*, p.57, Zimmermann mentions the use of birds as metaphorical images and observes that the blackbird was the first to be treated thus in Anglo-Irish songs. On p.119

he prints six verses of a song entitled "The Royal Blackbird" and the second verse agrees with Bunting's extract. The song appeared as an early 18th century broadside and remained popular throughout the 19th century. The earliest printed version appears to have been issued on a broadside in London, about 1718. In *Stanford-Petrie* there are four tunes which are variants of 'A Spailpín a Rúin' which in turn is a variant of 'The Blackbird': 292 — The Tumbling Down Teady's Acre; 519 — Along the Mourne Shore; 172 — The Reading Made Easy; 1379 — Spailpín Rúin!.]

99. CLÁRA de BÚRC
Clara Burke

TITLE: *1840, p.73:* Clara Burke. Index, p.III: Clara de Burc. Tune: MS.33, bk.I. p.39 "Clara Burke". No key signature and badly notated.

Tá sár-ghuth ceóil ag an leanbhán óg,
Go mo chrádh go mór le searc éiríos (?);
'S a cáble fhoilt ór-bhuidhe a' fás 'n-a deóidh
Go sála bróg i n-a gcamóigíní (?).

Ní breátha na deóir i mbarr na mór-chnoc
Lá bheadh reó nó leac oighre
Ná bláth na h-óige atá go fóill
I gcás bheith beó í na glan-mhaighdin (?).

Scríobh na déithe (?), draoithe 'gus éigse
Brí mo sgéil-se ar Chlára,
Gur shaoileas féin san oidhche aréir
Gurab í do leig mé i n-anbhfainn.

A naoidhe bheag bhéasach, mhaordha, shéimhidh,
Shighmigh (?), chéilligh, innealtaigh (?),
Agus do chliú do spreáchadh mar chlúmh n-éan
I dtús an lae ins a' Mhárta thall.

143

Tá a cúl trom triopallach, cuacach, cochallach,
Droimneach, femuineach (?), fréamh-ghlan, fionn;
Is ar a corp mar raidh (?) gheal nach bhfuil balamh (?),
Ach cumhra, soilbhir, séimh-ghlan, caoin.

TRANSLATION

1. The young maiden has the sweetest voice for singing, My love for her torments me greatly; Her golden-yellow tresses hang at her back, And down to her heels in ringlets. 2. No finer are the droplets on the hilltops Even on a frosty day Than the bloom of youth which is still Glowing in the pure maiden. 3. Let the gods, druids and poets Tell what I think of Clara, And last night it seemed to me That it was she who had left me without strength. 4. O small, mannerly, noble, gentle maid, (?), sensible and lively, Your face used to shine like the bird's plumage At daybreak on a March day. 5. Her hair is thick in clusters, curled and ringleted, Toppling, (?), clear and fair, And on her body as a ? ? ? But sweet-scented, pleasing, clean and gentle.

NOTES

AIR: Noted from Mrs. Burke at Carrakeel, Co. Mayo on 1792.

WORDS: MS.7 No.149 — presumably from the same source. The song consists of ten verses, but I have had to omit the first five as I find them practically unintelligible. The second five are not much better, as the number of queries indicates.

100. TÁIM I MO CHODHLADH IS NÁ DÚISIGH MÉ

TITLE: *1840, p.74:* I am asleep and don't waken me. Index p.VI: Ta me mo chodladh. Tune: MS.33, bk.3, pp.56/7: "From Hempson". Marked Allegro.

NOTES

[Noted from Hempson the harper at Magilligan in 1792. In the introduction p.95, Bunting writes:—

" 'Ta me mo dholadh. I am asleep, and don't waken me.' — An ancient and beautiful air, unwarrantably appropriated by the Scotch, among whom Hector O'Neill has written words to it. The Irish words are evidently very old, and consist only of six lines:

'I am asleep, without rocking, through this quarter of the night;
I am asleep, and do not waken me;
O kindly, dear mother, get up and make light for me,
For I am sick, and evil has happend me,' etc. etc."

O'Neill tells us the following curious anecdote connected with this tune. When at Mr. Macdonnell's of Knochranty in the county of Roscommon, he met a young nobleman from Germany who had come to Ireland to look after some property to which he had a claim through his mother. "He was one of the most finished and accomplished young gentlemen," says O'Neill, "that I ever met. When on one occasion Hugh O'Neill and I had played our last tunes for him, he wished to call for 'Past one o'clock', or 'Tha me mo chodladh, naar dhoesk a me,' which he had heard played somewhere before, but for the name of which he was at a loss. Perceiving me going towards the door, he followed me, and said that the name of his bootmaker was Tommy McCullagh, and that the tune he wanted was like saying 'Tommy McCullagh made boots for me;' and in the broad way he pronounced it, it was not unlike the Irish name. I went in with him and played it, on which he seemed uncommonly happy."

Anne Willis's edition of Neal's *Celebrated Irish Tunes* contains the following list of references:

Burk Thumoth's *Twelve Scotch and Twelve Irish Airs:* p.15 "Past one o'cloch'

Neal's *Collection of most Celebrated Irish Tunes,* p.12

Walker's *Historical Memoirs of the Irish Bards,* 32: "Ta me mo chodladh"

O'Farrell's *Pocket Companion for the Irish or Union Pipes,* I 68: "Past one o'clock". A copy of Walkers

Holden's *Collection of Old-Established Irish slow and quick tunes* II, 15: "Past one o'clock"

Holden's *Collection of Old-Established Irish slow and quick tunes* II, 35: "Thamama Hulla"

Mulholland's *Ancient Irish Airs,* 32: "Ta me ma chodhladh"

The Complete Collection of Irish Music edited from the Petrie MSS by Stanford, 488: "I am asleep and don't wake me"

O'Neill's *Music of Ireland,* 599: "Ta me mo chodladh". A copy of the Bunting tune.

Rough sketches of the tune are to be found in MS.28, pp.26/27. The words can be found in Walshe's *Ceól Ar Sínsear*, p.95.

In the *Journal of the Irish Folk Song Society*, Vol.I, p.16, C. Milligan Fox published a tune. "Lament of a Druid" which is a variant of 'Táimse im' Chodladh'. The note under the tune is as follows: "This plaintive lament was piped to me by Piper Kelly, an old musician who wanders round the North of Ireland. He said this lament was given to him by "ould Jimmy Joyce, a Galway piper", who had been to the Belfast Convention of Harpers in 1792."

Two other versions of the tune are to be found in the Goodman MSS. 1.8 and 3.47.]

101. CEANN DUBH DÍLIS

TITLE: *1840, p.75:* Black Headed Deary. Index, p.III: Cara chean dílí. Tune: MS.5, p.47 "Cean dubh dealish. From Thaydy Conalon." The words of the chorus are written under the ntoes of the second part of the tune.

WORDS: Hyde's *Love Songs of Connacht* 1931 Edition pp.45-46

Tá mná an bhaile seo ar buile 's ar buaidhreadh,
Ag tarraing a ngruaige 's 'gá leigean le gaoith.
Ní ghlacfaidh siad sgafair d'fhearaibh na tuaithe,
Go dtéidh siad 'san ruaig le buachaillibh an rígh.

Ceann dubh dílis dílis dílis,
Ceann dubh dílis, druid liom análl,
Ceann dubh is gile ná 'n eala 's an fhaoileann,
Is duine gan chroidhe nach dtiubhradh dhuit grádh.

A ógánaigh uasail uasail uasail,
Gheobhaidh tú duais a's fuirigh go lá.
Geobhaidh tú sgioból a's urlár an bhuailte,
Agus cead do bheith thuas go n-éirighe an lá.

Ceann dubh dílis dílis dílis,
Ceann dubh dílis, druid liom análl,
Ceann dubh is gile ná 'n eala 's an fhaoileann,
Is duine gan chroidhe nach dtiubhradh dhuit grádh.

TRANSLATION

1. The women of this place are distracted and furious, Pulling their hair and leaving it to the wind. They won't take a spruce fellow from the men of the country, Hoping for an adventure with the boys of the king. 2. Dear, dear, dear dark head, Dear dark head come hither with me, Dark head that is lovelier than the swan of the sea-gull, It is a heartless person that would not give you love. 3. Noble, noble, noble young man, You will get a reward if you tarry till day. You will get a barn and a threshing-floor, And leave to stay up till break of day. 4. Dear, dear, dear, dark head, etc.

NOTES

The Index p.VIII states that the piece was noted from "T. Conlan

in 1831." In the Introduction p.94/95 Bunting writes:—
"Cara ceann dílis. "Black-headed Dear"' — This ancient air has
hitherto been improperly set in a minor, instead of a major key.
A slight examination will prove that the setting now adopted bears
in itself strong marks of genuine originality. In a small collection
of Irish airs, published about 1726 by Neal, of Christ Church Yard,
Dublin, Cara Ceann Dilis is found in a minor key; and that setting
has been adopted by Burke Thumoth as well as by Oswald in his
"Caledonian Pocket Companion." But, as it is sung by the peasantry
to this day in the style and manner given in this work, the setting
here adopted is presumed to be correct. No Irish words can now be
found for the air, as set in a minor key."

[In MS.33, bk.5, p.15 ("Old way of 'Cean dubh dileash' ") is found
the copy on which Bunting based the printed version.
 The following list of references is taken from an edition of Neale's
Celebrated Irish Tunes, by Anne Willis:
 Durfey's *Pills to Purge Melancholy*, II, 14, "A Consolatory Ode
to Her Majesty"
 Neal's *Collection of the most Celebrated Irish Tunes*, p.16, "Can
dubh dilish"
 Wright's *Aria di Camera*, 62, "Can dubh dilich"
 Thompson's *Hibernian Muse*, 20, "Curri Kown Dilich"
 Walker's *Historical Memoirs of the Irish Bards*, 31, "Cur do cheann
dilis — Lay the dear head"
 Brysson's *Curious Selection of Favourite Tunes*, 19(a), "The Old
Jew"
 Holden's *Collection of Old-Established Irish Slow and Quick
Tunes*, II, 13, "Ceann Dubh Deelish".
 There are also three tunes with this title in Stanford-Petrie,
Nos, 1061, 1062, 1535; but of these only 1062 suits the words.
The tune is also in McFadden's *Repository of Scots and Irish Airs*
(c.1796).
 O'Neill refers to the tune in *Irish Folk Music*, p.191.]

WORDS: There are two copies which are very similar to each other;
Hardiman's *Irish Minstrelsy* Vol.I, p.262 and Hyde's *Love Songs of
Connacht*, p.45/46, which is printed above.

102. THE MINERS OF WICKLOW

TITLE: *1840, p.76:* The Miners of Wicklow. Index, p.IV: Mianairea Cille Meann-
táin. Tune: MS.13, p.109.

NOTES

[Obtained from "Macdonnell, piper in 1797". This is a typical double jig. Variants are to be found in O'Neill's *Dance Music of Ireland*, No.210; in Aird's *Selection of Scotch, English and Irish Airs*, Vol. I (c.1795) No.23; in McGown's *Repository of Scots and Irish Airs*, c.1800, and in Levey's *Dance Music of Ireland*, Vol.I, p.10.]

103. CHORUS JIG

TITLE: *1840, p.76:* Chorus Jig. Index p.III: Damhsa Loineach. Tune: MS.13, p.109.

NOTES

[As in the case of the previous tune the source is "Macdonnell, the piper in 1797". This piece is more in the nature of a reel rather than a jig, but if the rhythm is 'swung' slightly the meter changes to 12/8 time and the piece takes on the movement of a single jig. The metronome indication (quaver equals 88) suggests a single jig rather than a reel.

In O'Neill's *Dance Music of Ireland*, No.342 there is a double jig with the title "The Chorus Jig", not related to Bunting's tune.

In *Old Irish Folk Music and Songs* No.67 Joyce prints a tune under the same title and remarks that it is a "great favoorite with pipers". Again this is a variant of O'Neill's tune and bears no resemblance to Bunting's tune.

Two more versions of the O'Neill tune are to be found in Murphy's *Irish Airs and Jigs*, p.15 and in Holden's *Old Established Tunes*, Vol. I, p.24. O'Neill refers to the tune in *Irish Folk Music*, p.155.]

104. EDWARD DODWELL

TITLE: *1840, p.77*: Emon Dodwell. Index, III: Eamonn Dodbhall. Tune: MS.33, bk.3, p.21: "Emon Dabhal or Ned Dodwel. By Carolan." Key signature of one flat but every note B is marked natural.

Slán linn siar go bruach an chuain
Mar a bhfuil an suairc-fhear Éadbhaird
Dodbhaill sáimh, nach gnáth faoi ghruaim
    Do oidhche ná do ló.
Comhrádh ciúin is ráite tuigse,
Sé chuireadh cách uaidh ól an uisge,
Is móide m'adhbhar gluaiseacht aige,
    Agus triallamaoid gan spás.

Croidhe gan ghruaim i stuaim 's i dtuigse,
Planda uasal, lúthmhar, meisneamhail,
Súd mar tá sé, súgach, fáilteach,
    Is go bhfuil an chóige lán dá ghrádh.
Nach mór an sgéal é luighe leis féin,
Is a liachtaighe speirbhean mhúinte bhéasach
Súil le Éadbhaird theacht dá bhféáchaint
    'Tabhairt grinn is siansa dhóibh!

TRANSLATION

1. Good-bye to us westwards to the brink of the bay Where resides the affable man Edward Dodwell the pleasant, who is never out of humour By night or by day. Quiet of converse and intelligent of speech. 'Tis he would have everyone drinking his whisky. I have good reason to call on him, And I shall set off without delay. 2. Heart without gloom, modest and understanding, Noble scion, nimble and courageous, That is what he is, humorous and hospitable, And the province is full of his affection. Is it not strange that he lies alone, When there are so many lovely girls, educated and polite, Hoping that Edward will come to see them, Giving them pleasure and delight!

AIR: Noted by Bunting from Charles Byrne the harper in 1792. The tune as printed in the *1840* volume is an inferior version and is to be found in MS.33 bk.5, p.78. See *DOSC* I p.186 and II, p.26.

WORDS: From Thaddeus Connellan's *An Duaniare (Fonna Seanma),* 1829. Other versions of the words are in *Amhráin Cearbhalláin,* by Ó Máille, and in MS.17, p.29, and MS.10, No.9.

Connellan's title is "Edward Dodwell, Esq., County Sligo: by Carolan". If so, he must have been one of the Dodwell's of Mount Dodwell in that county. All that can be gathered from the poem is that he was a bachelor and lived by the shore. But this is not true of Mount Dodwell. But the Dodwell's had another estate in County Galway, at Portumna, which is on the shore or Lough Derg, the second largest lake in Ireland; and the subject of this piece may have belonged to this branch of the family.

105. A MHUIRNÍN
My Darling

TITLE: *1840, p.77:* The Darling. Index, p.I: A muirnin. Tune: *1840, p.77.*

NOTES

Noted from Denis Hempson, the harper, at Magilligan, County Derry in 1796.

I have found no other version of this piece.

152

106. AN SEANDUINE SPAD-CHLUASACH
The old man with drooped ears

TITLE: *1840, p.78:* The deaf old man. Index, p.II: An seanduine spad chluasach. Tune: MS.33, bk.4, p.2: Marked by Bunting "Very good".

NOTES
[Noted from "Mrs Fitzgerald, Westport, 1802". The tune is also to be found in MS.6, p.80 with the words of a song entitled "An Bata" with the note "ar fonn (to the air or) an tsean duine spaod chluasach". This tune is the same as the version in MS.33, except that Bars VI and XVI are written as follows:]

107. MISS HAMILTON

TITLE: *1840, p.79:* Miss Hamilton. Index, p.V: Neeni Hamilton. Tune: MS.33, bk.3, p.41: "From Hugh Higgins. Composed by Lyons, harper to Lord Antrim. Lyons was contemporary with Carolan."

153

NOTES

According to the Index, p.IX, this piece was composed by Cornelius Lyons, harper to the Earl of Antrim, in 1706. It was noted from Patrick Linden the harper in 1802 (Index, p.IX). The MS. however gives Hugh Higgins as the source.

Bunting has the following comment on page 99 of his Introduction: "Remarkable as being the composition of the last of the old race of Irish harpers. It is a piece of Lyons's, but to what Miss Hamilton it was addressed the Editor is not aware, through the probability is that she was one of the Killeagh family. None of the successors of Lyons attempted to compose an air; their utmost effort was a meagre attempt at arrangment."

Also, on page 70, he quotes an amusing story about Lyons and his patron. "His lordship was both a wit and a poet, and delighted in equality where vulgarity was not too gross. At one time he and Lyons, when in London, went to the house of a famous Irish harper named Heffernan, who kept a tavern there; but beforehand they formed the following plan. 'I will call you Cousin Burke', said his lordship. 'You may call me either Cousin Randall or My Lord, as you please.' After regailing for some time, Heffernan was

154

called up, who was by this time well aware of the dignity of his host from the conversation and livery of his lordship's servants. When Heffernan came into the room he was desired to bring in his harp and sit down, which he did, and played a good many tunes in a grand style. His lordship then called upon his cousin Burke to play a tune. The supposed cousin, after many apologies, at length took the harp and played some of his best airs. Heffernan, after listening a little while, started up and exclaimed, 'My lord, you may call him Cousin Burke, or what cousin you please, but *dar Dhia* [by God] he plays upon Lyons's fingers.' What is very extraordinary, Heffernan had never seen Lyons before. His lordship then retired, leaving the minstrels to indulge in Bacchanalian rivalry."

[In Oswald's *Caledonian Pocket Companion* IV, p.17, there is a variant entitled 'The Blossom of the Raspberry' with two further variation-type sections added and culminating in a 6/8 'Gig' tune.]

108. BALTIGHORAN

TITLE: *1840, p.79:* Baltighoran. Index p.II: Baltigh Abhran. Introduction p.94 title referred to as 'Baltiorum'. Tune: MS.5, p.38: "Baal Tighe Abhrán, le Tadhg Ó Coinnialáin, 1833. The Song of the House of Baal."

NOTES

[Noted from "T. Conlan in 1831" (Index p.VII). A four-part variant under the title "Baulthy Oura" is in O'Farrell's *Pocket Companion*, Vol. IV, p.108. Another variant is in Joyce's *Old Irish Folk Music and Songs*, No.697 ("Baltyoran").

In *The English Dialet of Donegal*, a glossary incorporating the collections of H.C. Hart M.R.I.A. (1847-1908) by Michael Traynor, the following entry is to be found: "*Baltiorum*: A form of dance. Is it a reel or a jig or a Baltiorum?"]

109. BONNY PORTMORE

TITLE: *1840, p.109:* Bonny Portmore. Index, p.V: Peggi Ni Leavan. Tune: MS.33, bk.3, p.61: "Pegy Ní Shleibhe or Peggy na Leavien. Noted from Arthur O'Neill." But in the Index of *1840* it is stated to have been obtained from Daniel Black, the harper, at Glenoak in 1796.

I have found no variants, and nothing is known of the girl, whose name is wrongly spelt in Irish and would be in English Peggy or Margaret Levinge. Bunting has the following note on p.97 of his Introduction:

"A favourite air in the country about Ballinderry, in the county of Antrim. Portmore, an old residence of the O'Neills, stood on the banks of Lough Beg, a small and shallow, but picturesque, sheet of water adjoining Lough Neagh. The ivy-clad ruins of the old church still stand on a neighbouring eminence, which in summer forms a promontory, and in winter is surrounded by the waters of the lake. On the plantation of this part of the country in 1611, Portmore became the property of Lord Conway, who built a mansion here, of which there are still some traces. This was a favourite retreat of Doctor Jeremy Taylor, when Bishop of Dromore; and the tree under which he used to sit, to hear this melody sung by the peasantry was pointed out until some years ago. The air is probably as old as the time of the O'Neills of Ballinderry, to whose declining fortunes there would appear to be an allusion in the first stanza of the English words, which are still sung with it:

Bonny Portmore, you shine where you stand
And the more I think on you the more my heart warms.
But if I had you now, as I had once before,
All the gold in all England would not buy you, Portmore!

[For another version see *The Irish Song Tradition*, p.51 (Dublin, 1976) by Seán O'Boyle.]

110. THE CUCKOO'S NEST

TITLE: *1840, p.81:* The Cuckoo's Nest. Index, p.IV: Nead na cuaiche. Tune: 1840, p.81.

NOTES

[Bunting states in the Index p.X that he got this piece from "an old music book of 1723" This tune was used by the 18th century Munster poet Eoghan Rua Ó Súilleabháin for his poem "An Spealadóir".

Two more settings are to be found in O'Neill's *Music of Ireland*, Nos.1733 and 1734. The latter is also in O'Neill's *Dance Music of Ireland*, (No.913).

A version is also to be found in *Stanford-Petrie*, No.1206. In Aird's *Scotch, English, Irish and Foreign Airs*, Vol.I, No.190, there is a variant entitled "Come ashore Jolly Tar".]

111. BRÍD ÓG NA gCIABH

TITLE: *1840, p.82:* Young Bridget. Index p.II: Bríghid Óg na gciabh. Tune: MS.33, bk.5, p.4 and MS.33, bk.I, p.5.

WORDS: MS.18, p.55 and MS.7, No.67

A Bhríd Óg na gciabh bréagh daithe, mo mhian,
'S gur gile thú ná grian an fhómhair;
'S gur dtroiscfinn leat bliadhain mhór fhada ar a' tsliabh,
Gan tine, gan bia 'n-ár gcomhair.
Ó d'imthigh tú i gcian 's i bhfad as mo líon,
'S nach bhfillidh tú i ndéidh an Domhnaigh,
Níl dhomhsa 'dó dhiadh, mar d'athraigh tú ciall,
Ach mo fhortún bheith ar Rí na Glóire.

Tá siad dhá rádh go bhfuil tú 's mé i ngradh,
'S go dtuilleann(?) tú gráin ró-mhór dhom;

Feasta go brách ní leagfad mo lámh
Ar bhean ar bith go bhfaighid mé dóigh cheart.
Is agamsa tá an drámh, is neasa do mhádh,
'S an cuireat, gan trácht ar aon truich;
's an té nach bhfuair cárta riamh daithe 'n-a láimh,
Faigheann sé bruinneall gan smál le breágadh.

Tá grádh agam ar mhnaoi gaus is ainm di Bríd,
'S ar dhuine nó ar dhís ní shéanfad;
'S gur bí siúd mo mhian thar mhnáibh deasa 'n tsaoil,
'S go bhfuil 'fhios ag an tír nach bréag é.
Tá geataí na saoithe 'dul eadram a's í,
'S ná feadaim-se dhul d'á féachaint;
Fan agam-sa oídhche, ráithe nó mí,
'S a charaid mo chroidhe, ná tréigh mé!

TRANSLATION

1. Young Bridget of the fair bright tresses, my darling, You are brighter than autumn sun; And I would fast with you for a great long year on the mountain, Without a fire near us, or food. Since you went away, far from my net, And will not come back after Sunday, I shall not follow you, unless you change your mind, But my fortune will be for the King of Glory. 2. They are saying that you and I are in love, And that you hate me exceedingly; Henceforward for ever I shall not give my hand To any woman unless I get encouragement. It is I have the useless card, next to the trump, And the knave, not to mention the ace of clubs; And the man who never got a coloured card in his hand, He gets a spotless maid for courting. 3. I am in love with a woman named Bridget, And I will not deny that to one or two; And she is my choice of the world's lovely woman, And everybody knows that is true. The gates of the wise come between me and her, And I cannot go to see her; Stop with me a night, a quarter or a month, And, sweetheart, don't desert me!

NOTES

AIR: Noted by Bunting in 1792 from "an old man at Deel Castle". The opening bars are noted in pencil in MS.5 p.34. Some MSS. (not Bunting's) mention this song as being a composition by Carolan. It is, therefore, dealt with in full in *DOSC* I p.180 and *DOSC* II p.21/22.

WORDS: These were noted by Patrick Lynch from Nat Guttery, Castlebar. These verses have a folk ring about them and they do not seem characteristic of Carolan. The MS. does not attribute them to him.

Five quatrains are printed in *Amhráin Cearbhalláin* (Ó Máille p.233 plus some additional lines which do not appear to belong to the song. One of the MSS. from which the words in *Amhráin Cearbhalláin* were printed has 'Carolan cct.' and another is headed 'fourth Song for Bridget Cruise'. But the style is unlike that of Carolan, and the song is attributed to Seamus Mac Caurta in Murray's edition of that poet, p.80.

112. MacDONNELL'S MARCH

TITLE: *1840*, p.83: Macdonnell's March. Index, p.IV: Mairseail Alasdroin.
Tune: MS.33, bk.2, p.74: "Aulestrums March. Anno 1647. March of the
Munster Pipers."

NOTES

On pp.91-92 of his Introduction Bunting has a long introduction
to this air, as follows:

"This air is mentioned in a note to Smith's *History of Cork,* Vol.
II, p.159 in the following words: 'There is a very odd kind of music
well known in Munster by the name of MacAllisdrum's March,
being a wild rhapsody made in honor of this commander, to this day
much esteemed by the Irish and played at all their feasts'." Bunting
continues: "This was Alister or Alexander Macdonnell, son of Coll
Kittogh [Ciotach] or Left-handed Coll, a warrier whose name has
been preserved by Milton:
　Why, it is harder, Sirs, than Gordon,
　Colkittor, or MacDonnell, or Galasp.
And even more imperishably by vivid traditions of his valour and
prowess, handed down to this day, among the Highlanders of Scotland
and the glensmen of the lower part of the county of Antrim. Alister,
called also 'Young Colkitto', rivalled his father in military fame.
He commanded Lord Antrim's Irish, under Montrose, to most of
whose victories his courage and conduct mainly contributed. After
the breaking up of Montrose's army, Macdonnell and his Irish re-

161

turned to this country and joined the standard of the confederate Catholics under Lord Taaffe in Munster, where a period was put to their exploits by the fatal battle of Knockinoss, 28th September, 1647. After the rout of the main body of the Irish, Macdonnell and his people held their ground till they were cut to pieces by the English. It is said that none escaped. We may form some idea of the desperate courage which inspired these men from the impetuous energy and wild shrilly fervour of this strain, which is undoubtedly the same *pibroch* [*píobaireacht* — pipe tune] that they marched to on the morning of their last battle. Macdonnell himself lies buried near Kanturk, in the county of Cork, and his sword, which had a steel apple running in a groove on the back, by means of which its force in striking was greatly increased, is said still to be preserved in Loghan Castle, in the county of Tipperary."

[This piece is a section of a longer descriptive piece for the pipes entitled "Mairséail Alasdruim". Breandán Breathnach deals with it in detail in the journal *Ceol*, volume III Nos. 2 and 3, where he prints versions from the Goodman MSS., from an essay written in 1876 by Francis Keane and from various 19th Century MSS. The piece is also in Crofton Croker's *Researches in the South of Ireland* (1824) and the oldest reference is to be found in a MS. collection compiled in Lisronagh near Clonmel, Co. Tipperary, in 1784 and now in the possession of Eoghan Ó Néill.

Bunting got this tune from "a piper at Westport, 1802" (Index p.IX).]

113. THE WILD GEESE

TITLE: *1840, p.84:* The Wild Geese. Index, p.IV: Géadna Fiadhaine. Tune: MS.33, bk.1, p.67.

NOTES

Noted from Patrick Quin, the harper, in 1803. There are versions in Thompson's *Hibernian Music* (c.1789): Irish Air; *Holden's collection*, Vol.II (1806): Gage Fane, which is obviously intended for "Na Géana Fiadhaine", Irish for "The Wild Geese"; and *Mulholland's Collection* (1810), under the wrong title of "The Wild Swan", Holden's version was used by Moore for his song "Tis believed that this harp" in the third number of the *Melodies* (1810). [There is a version in Neale's *Celebrated Irish Tunes*, p.25. The tune can also be found in MS.29, p.68, which is a transcription of sections of the tune from "a printed book". The final fourteen bars of the piece are a development of the last two bars of the second phrase.]

In his Introduction to the *1840* volume, p.93, Bunting states of this tune: "It was composed as a farewell to the gallant remnant of the Irish army, who, upon the capitulation of Limerick in 1691, preferred an honourable exile to remaining in the country when their cause was lost, and who afterwards so well sustained the national reputation, under the name of the Irish Brigade, in the Continental wars. It is commonly believed that the air was sung by the women assembled on the shore at the time of the embarkation."

163

The words "gallant remnant" are somewhat misleading in view of the numbers involved. The exodus was, of course, gradual; but it is stated in MacGeoghan's *History of Ireland*, p.599, that "within the 50 years which followed the Treaty of Limerick 450,000 Irish soldiers *died* (my italics) in the service of France".

It might be added that Bunting's Irish title, *Na Géadna Fiadhaine*, is a mere translation of the English. Even those who did not know English (the vast majority of the people at that time) used the term "Wild Geese", which was appropriate because these militant emigrants flocked together in concert before taking their flight.

The point is illustrated in an elegy made by a native of West Cork for his three sons and a son-in-law — fishermen wrecked on Carraig Aonair (the Lone Rock), which is four and a half miles south-west of Cape Clear, the most southerly point of Ireland. The Fastnet Lighthouse now stands on it. One of the verses runs:

'sé mo chreach is mo dhíth nár leigeas iad ar luing
I gcomhar le Saoi Séamus mar a dtéadh na *Wild Geese*:
Bheadh mo shúil-se le Críost le n-a gcumann arís,
Is nárbh í Carraig Aonair ba chéile dhom chloinn.

This means: "Ah! woe is me that I did not let them go aboard ship along with Sir James in the wake of the Wild Geese! Then I would have hoped in Christ for their society again, And that the Lone Rock would not be the spouse of my children."

The full text of this touching poem, with the tune, 11 verses and a translation, appears in my *Songs of the Irish* (1960), pp.83-85. The Sir James mentioned is probably Sir James FitzEdmund Cotter, of Anngrove, County Cork. He was a distinguished adherent of the Stuarts and slew the regicide John Lisle at Lausanne in 1664. He commanded for the King in Munster during the Cromwellian war and led his men to France after the Capitulation of Limerick in 1691.

114. AN NÓINÍN CONNACHTACH
The Connaught Daisy

TITLE: *1840, p.85:* The Connaught Daisy. Index, p.V: Nóinín Conachtach.
Tune: MS.5, p.60: "Connaught Daisy from Coady".

NOTES

The printed tune was noted from Hugh Higgins the harper, in 1792. It would appear to be a harp-melody rather than a song-air. At any rate there are no words for it in the MSS.

[The MS. version above, was noted from James Coady who was a piper. It bears little resemblance to the Hugh Higgins version but both tunes can be seen to be related through similarities of title, meter, rhythm and phrase lengths. The overall length, number of phrases and modality of the tunes are different.

The Hugh Higgins version appears to be related also to "An Bonnáin Buí" p.56 in the *1840* collection.]

115. SLIGO TUNE

TITLE: *1840, p.86:* Sligo Tune. Index, p.I: Abhrán Shligigh. Tune: MS.5, p.45: "Ancient Irish Air — name unknown. From Mrs. Blest of Co. Sligo."

[The index, p.X gives the source as "an old woman in Sligo, 1802". The title of the tune is obviously Bunting's own (see MS. note above). In the Intro. p.95, Bunting writes:— "The first bar of this ancient tune is like the Scotch song 'Will you go to the Ewe boughts Marion'; the wildness of the melody is remarkable though not without merit." Bunting arranged the tune as a Canon in the *1840* volume. The Note A occurs only once in the published version and is natural. The key signature should therefore be two flats, placing the tune in the aeolian mode as in the case of the MS. version above. The B natural in bar four of the *1840* tune was inserted by Bunting for harmonic reasons.]

116. AN É AN SAGART?

TITLE: *1840, p.86:* Is is the priest you want. Index, p.V: Sagart 'ne an Sagart? Tune: MS.33, bk.2, p.45: "Nean saghart noin sagart or its the priest the priest you want. Ballinrobe."

NOTES

[Noted at Ballinrobe in 1792. This tune is related to "A Dhonnchadh Ná Bí Fogarthach" in Bunting's *1796 Collection*, p.10, No.20 and also in his *1809 Collection*, p.41. It is dealt with extensively in *DOSB* I, p.69/70.]

117. SLOANS LAMENTATION

TITLE: *1840, p.87:* Sloans lamentation. Index, p.I: Abhrán Shlóin. Tune: MS.5, pp.40/41: "W. Sloan's Tune".

NOTES

[Noted from "W. Sloane Esq. Armagh, 1800". By altering the final note of the first, second and fourth phrases Bunting changed an ionian tune (MS. version above) into an aeolian tune (the *1840* version).

"The foggy dew" (No.150 in the *1840 Collection*) is a variant of this tune.

Another variant, again with the title "The Foggy Dew", is to be found in the *Journal of the Irish Folk Song Society*, Vol.III, p.33.]

118. O MOLLY MY DEAR

TITLE: *1840, p.87:* O Molly my dear. Index, p.V: *Ó Máire Dhilis. Tune: 1840,* p.87: "O Molly Dear".

167

WORDS: MS.12, bk.I, p.68

O Molly my dear, I hear you're getting a man.
It would make my heart ache to see your wedding go on.
For fear of a fall, recall your senses in time,
For in spite of them all, sweet charming Molly, you're mine!

NOTES

The MS. copy is in MS.33, bk.2, p.70, and it is in 3/8 time. Bunting has written at the foot of the page: "This must be in 9/8 "and adds the date: "28th October 1807". The key is much too high for singing and so I have copied the tune from the *1840* volume, which is otherwise identical.

[His MS. title is "If you were shaved you would make a handsome young man". Thomas Moore used this tune for his song "At the mid-hour of night". The Index p.IX gives the source as "Patrick Quin, harper, 1800".

To fit the words to the tune it is necessary to omit one phrase of the tune, preferably the second. This would give the tune an ABBA form. The MS. version is, in fact, written out in this form but with a repeat mark after the first phrase.]

119. AN CHÚILFHIONN
The Fair-haired One

TITLE: *1840, p.88:* Coolin or Lady of the Desert. Index, p.III: Cuilin. Tune: MS.33, bk. 2, p.1: "Coolin or Lady of the Desert. Very ancient. Got (or "get") the words from Mrs. Conner." There follows, on pp.2 and 3, four variations by Lyons, noted from Hempson. These are in the *1840* volume.

WORDS: MS.11, p.30

Dá bhaicfeá-sa an chúilionn,
Is í siúl ar na bóithribh
Dul bealach na cúl-choill'
'S an drúcht lena brógaibh.

Mo bhrón 'sí mo rún í
Is níl [tnuth?] aici le óige,
'S go dtug sí barr múinte
Ar chúigíbh na Fódla.

Is lonrach 's is péarlach
An mhaighdean chiúin tséimh í,
Is ró-dheise len fhéachaint
'Na scéimh an ghréinéirí(?).

Samhail de Dheirdre
A méin is a breáthacht
Mar shoilse lae ag éirí
Nó réalta oíche Márta.

TRANSLATION

1. If you were to see the fair lady, As she walked the roads Going by the way of the back woods And the dew on her shoes. 2. Alas, she is my loved one And she pities not my youth She excels the five provinces of Erin In high accomplishments. 3. She is radiant and beautiful This mild gentle maiden It is a great loveliness to see In her beauty, the rising sun. 4. She is an image of Venus In her disposition and splendour As the morning light arising Or as the stars on a March sky.

NOTES

[Noted from "Hempson, at Magilligan in 1796". The Index p.VIII states "very ancient with variations by Lyons in 1700". These variations are to be found in MS.33, bk.2, pp.2 and 3.

In the Intro. p.89/90, Bunting writes:— "This far-famed melody is here given as it was played by Hempson who had learned his set

169

of it, with variations from Lyons."

Flood makes some references to this piece in his *History of Irish Music*, pp.87 and 108. See also Hardiman's *Irish Minstrelsy*, Vol.I, p.250 and 349. Here is a list of the main occurences of the tune in other collections:

Walker's *Irish Bards*, part X, p.8 (1786)
McFadden's *Scotch, English, Irish and Foreign Airs*, Vol. V, p.29 (1790-7)
O'Farrell's *National Pipe Music*, p.33 (1797-1800)
O'Farrell's *Pocket Companion*, No.122 (1801-10)
Holden's *Old Established Tunes*, p.28 (1806-7)
Murphy's *Irish Airs and Jigs*, p.8 (1809)
Kinloch's *100 Airs*, No.25 (c.1815)
Hime's *Pocket Book*, p.33 (c.1810)
Mooney's *History of Ireland*, p.532 (1846)
Joyce's *Irish Music and Song*, No.564 (1888)
Stanford's edition of the *Petrie MSS*, Nos. 598/599 (1905)

Some additional references and information may be found in Luke Donnellon's article 'The Coulin' in the *County Louth Archaeological Journal*, Vol. 3 (1912-1915), p.11.

An indication of the popularity of this air may be seen from the following selected references found in the sheet-music collection in the National Library of Ireland:

The favourite air of Coolin with variations for the pedal harp or pianoforte composed and dedicated to Miss Sarah Browne (of Mount Prospect) by a friend, Dublin, n.d.
Coolin, A favourite Irish air with variations, Dublin, J.Lee (c. 1785; with guitar part)
Coolin with words. A much admired Irish song. (Beginning: "Oh! the hours I have pass'd in the arms of my dear"; with piano accompaniment, and also arranged for guitar). Dublin, J. Hill, 1787
Coolun with variations. And the favourite Irish air of Candudelish, Dublin, J. McCalley (c.1790)
Coolun. A celebrated Irish air with variations [and] Caun du dellish. A favourite Irish air: with variations, Dublin, Hime (c. 1795)
Coolun. A celebrated Irish air to which is added variations for the pianoforte, violin, German flute and guitar, London, published for T. Skillern (c. 1800)
Coolun with variations for the flute, pianoforte and violin [also with arrangement for harp] , Edinburgh, Penson and Robertson (c.1823).]

120. CARRICKMACROSS AIR

TITLE: *1840, p.91:* Carrickmacross Air. Index p.1: Aedhear charraic mhic chroise. Tune: MS.33, bk.2, p.35: "Got this tune at Carrickmacross. From . . . in March, 1794 . . . ." A piano accompaniment is included.

NOTES

[The Index p.VIII gives the source as "An old woman at Dundalk, 1794". As in the case of "Sligo tune" No.115, in this edition the title is undoubtedly Bunting's own. (See MS. note above).]

121. SÍLE BHEAG NÍ CHONNALÁIN

See *No. 49* in this edition.

122. CUMHA AN DÉ-BHEAN SÍ
The Lament of the Fairy Goddess

TITLE: *1840, p.92:* Cooee en Devenish or The Lamentation of Youths. Index, p.III: Cumha an Deibhinis. Tune: *1840*, pp. 92/93.

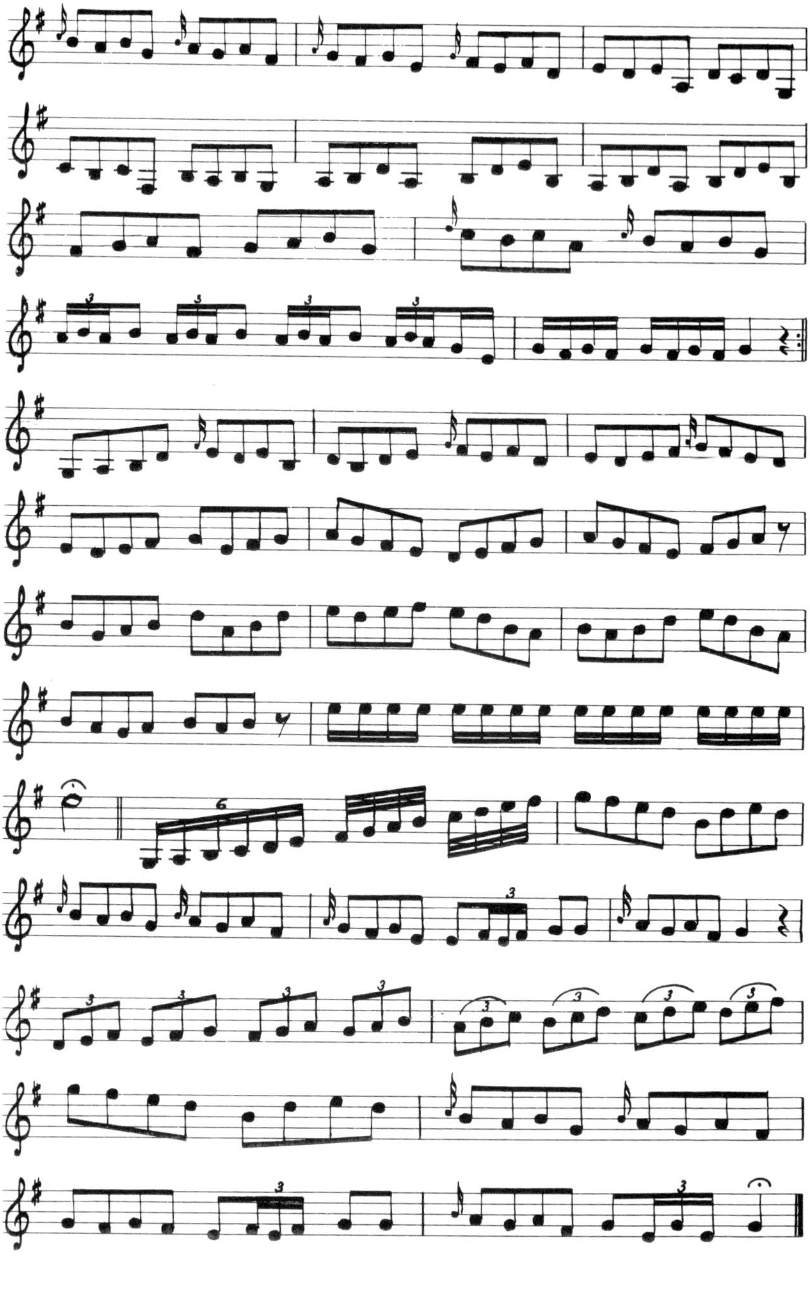

NOTES

[Noted from "D. O'Donnell, harper at Foxford, 1802". In the Introduction p.91, Bunting writes: "Another Caoine of Scott's, composed in memory of Hussey, Baron of Galtrim, who died A.D. 1603. It also consists of three parts or divisions, and abounds with those peculiar graces of performance alluded to in Chapter II. The Editor noted it down from the performance of Dominic O'Donnell, a harper from Foxford, in Mayo, who appeared totally unconscious of the art with which he was playing. This air differs from the preceding Caoine [No. 8 in this collection] by embracing all the intervals of the diatonic scale."

In the Index, p.XI and at the head of the piece (p.92) the piece is attributed to "Harry Scott in 1603". However in the note in the Intro. Bunting seems to suggest that the piece was composed by John Scott who composed "Scott's Lamentation for the Baron of Loughmoe" (No. 8 in this edition).

On p.69 of the Intro. Bunting writes: "Contemporary with O'Cahan were John and Harry Scott, two brothers born in the County of Westmeath, both eminent composers and performers. They were particularly distinguished for their "Caoinans" or dirge pieces. In this line they have produced pathetic movements for Purcell, Baron of Loughmoe, and O'Hussey, Baron Galtrim"

Bunting's translation of the title appears to be incorrect and a suggestion as to the correct form is given above.

An analysis of this piece shows it to be divided (like No.8) into three sections. Section I has sixteen bars and is heptatonic. Section II has twelve bars and is hexatonic, and Section III has ten bars and is heptatonic. The entire piece is based on a gradual 'rise and fall' movement through the use of sequential four-note quaver motives which themselves are made up of 'rise and fall' patterns as follows:—

ASCENDING FIGURE: This occurs in all sections.

DESCENDING FIGURE: Used in Sections II and III only

FALL, RISE, FALL:

In this figure the first fall and rise always involves the same interval whether it be a major or minor second. This is the principal figure in Section I. It occurs only twice in Section II and is used more often than any other in Section III. It is used mostly in sequential patterns involving a downward movement of the music.

RISE, RISE, FALL:

Used in Sections I and III only. In Section I it is used in an upward moving sequential pattern.

FALL, RISE, RISE:

This figure occurs in Section II only, where it is used in an upward moving sequential pattern.

There is one example in Section II, bar 10 of a 'Fall, Fall, Rise' movement.

As in the case of No.8 in this edition, the final note is emphasised at the cadence of each section. This is done through rapid reiteration of the note or through ornamenting it. In Section II, the music is basically involved in moving from a low tonic to a high submediant through the use of the figures mentioned. Section III is made up of a four-bar phrase repeated and each time preceded by a rapid ascending scale-like passage. Sections I and III are in the ionian mode while Section II has an aeolian cadence and emphasises the submediant throughout.

An even quaver pattern links the entire piece. The only let-up of this persistent quaver movement, apart from the main cadential points, is a quaver rest which gives an effect like the taking of a breath. This occurs twice in Section I and twice in Section II. A fair copy of the piece is to be found in MS.27, p.40. It is almost identical to the *1840* version except that the four-bar phrase in Section III is not repeated, and neither is it preceded by an ascending glissando-like passage. Neither does it contain the musical terminology printed by Bunting above the stave throughout the published version. All of these terms appear in the "General Vocabulary of Ancient Irish Musical Terms", pp.30-36 of the *1840* Introduction, and are marked "from the information of Arthur O'Neill etc." They are also to be found, with musical illustrations, in the Introduction

174

pp.24-28 under the heading "Graces Performed by the Treble or Left Hand".]

123. EILIONÓIR A RÚIN

TITLE: *1840, p.94*: Ellen a Roone. Index, p.III: Eibhlín a Rúin. Tune: MS.33, bk.2, pp.6/7 "Eibhleen a rúin — with variations by Lyons. From Denis Hempson. This set is quite different from any I ever met with."

WORDS: MS. 7, No. 114

"A' dtiocfadh tú nó a' bhfanadh tú,
Eilionóir a rúin?
A' dtiocfadh tú nó a' bhfanadh tú,
Eilionóir a rúin?"

176

"Tiocfadh mé 's ní fhanfadh mé,
A' gcreideann tú a gcana mé?
Seól romham mar leanfadh mé,
Grádh mo chroidhe thú!"

"Sheólfainn-se na gamhna leat,
Eilionóir a rúin.
Sheolfainn-se na gamhna leat,
Eilionóir a rúin.
Sheolfainn-se na gamhna leat
Síos go Tír Amhlaigh ar fad,
I ndúil go mbéinn i gcleamhnas leat,
Eilionóir a rúin!"

TRANSLATION

1. "Will you come or will you stay, Eleanor, my beloved? Will you come or will you stay, Eleanor, my beloved?" I shall come, I shall not stay, Do you believe what I am saying? Lead me and I shall follow, You are my heart's love!" 2. "I shall drive the cows with you, Eleanor my beloved, I shall drive the cows with you Right down to Tyrawley, In the hope that I shall wed you, Eleanor, my beloved!"

NOTES

[Noted from "Denis Hempson at Magilligan in 1792". In Vol. II, p.210 and p.264 of *Irish Minstrelsy*, Hardiman published two poems entitled 'Eibhlín a Rúin' ascribing the first one to a 14th century poet, and the second to a 17th century poet, both having the name Cearbhall Ó Dálaigh. In *Éigse*, Vol. XVIII, part 1 (1980), James E. Doan in an article 'The Poetic Tradition of Cearbhall Ó Dálaigh', concludes that there were several poets of that name between the 13th and the 17th centuries, and suggests that what we are dealing with in the modern Irish folk and literary tradition is in reality a composite *persona* made up of elements from all these poets.

The Bunting poem, at any rate, is related to Hardiman's 17th century version. Denis Hempson's tune, as it stands, does not fit either of the two basic versions, even though the one ascribed to the 14th century has four extra lines per verse. The MS. tune is not symmetrical on account of Bars 29 and 30. An acceptable solution would be to telescope both bars into one to form a bar of three groups of four semiquavers.

There is an extensive essay entitled 'Eibhlín a Rúin' by Luke Donnellan in the *County Louth Archaeological Journal* (1911) pp.417-425.

The following is a list of the principal occurrences of the tune: *The Beggar's Wedding* — a Ballad Opera by Charles Coffey, an Irishman, written in emulation of Gay's *Beggar's Opera*. It was performed in 1728 and contains the earliest version of 'Eibhlín a Rúin.'

McFadden's *Scotch, English, Irish and Foreign Airs*, Vol. V, p.29 (1790-1797)

O'Farrell's *Music for the Union Pipes*, p.30 (1797-1800)
Kinloch's *100 Airs*, No. 10, Part I (c.1815)
Burk Thumoth — *12 Scotch and Irish Airs*, No. XIII (c.1745-50)
O'Farrell's *Pocket Companion* p.20 (1801-10)
Murphy's *Irish Airs and Jigs* p.27 (1809)
Holden's *Old Established Tunes*, p.29 (1806-7)
Brysson's *Curious Selection* p.20 (c.1790)
Hime's *Pocket Book* p.16, Vol. IV (1810)
'Spirit of the Nation', p.15 (1846)
Mooney's *History of Ireland*, p.535 (1846)
Fáinne an Lae, 10th February (1900)
Ceol ár Sínsear, Rev. P. A. Walsh, Part V, p.18 (1920).
There are also references to the song in Flood's *History of Irish Music*, p.73 and p.249, and in the Introduction to Bunting's *1840* collection, p.90.
Additional notes are in Moffat's *Minstrelsy of Ireland*; the *Journal of the Irish Folk Song Society*, Vol. IX, p.16; and O'Neil's *Irish Folk Music* pp.164-168.
For information on Lyons, see No.107, 'Miss Hamilton', in this edition.
The piece consists of an eight-bar first section with a twelve-bar second section which is repeated with a variation where the piece reaches its first climax. A variation of Section I is then followed by two more variations of Section II with the piece reaching its final climax towards the end of the second variation.
In *Éigse*, Vol. II, p.208, in an article 'The Earliest Version of Eibhlín A Rúin', R.A. Breathnach gives a version of the words from a mid-18th century MS. The intersting thing about this text is that each verse contains an additional two lines over the usual version. If we take the first twenty bars of Hempson's piece as representing the basic tune, then the tune and text fit — allowing for some minor problems due to the instrumental nature of the music.
Here is the first verse:

> Móra agus Muire dhuit
>   A Eilín a rúin,
> Mora agus Muire dhuit,
>   A Eilín a rúin,
> Cúig mhíle Móra dhuit,
> Sé mhíle Móra dhuit,
>   Seacht míle, ocht míle,
> Naoi míle Móra dhuit,
> Móra agus Muire d[h]uit,
>   'Eilín a rúin!

The following references occur in the sheet-music collection of The National Library of Ireland:

Aileen Aroon made a duett, introduced by Miss Catley and Miss Wewitzer in the Beggar's Opera [beginning: "A curse attends that woman's love], Dublin, n.d.

Aileen Aroon: A favourite Irish song as sung by Sigr. Daudi at the Rotunda [beginning: Ducato non vanatu], Dublin, Sam Lee (c.1770)

Variations on Aileen Aroon for the harpsichord, violin, German flute and guitar, Dublin, John Lee (c.1790)

Aileen Aroon. A much admir'd Irish song [beginning: Ducatu non vanatu], Dublin, Hime (c.1795)

Aileen Aroon, with variations for the pianoforte or harpsichord, Dublin, Hime (c.1795)

Aileen Aroon, the original Irish melody from which was taken the popular ballad of Robin Adair, with variations for the harp, London, Clementi and Co. (c.1815)

Aileen Aroon, a favourite air as sung at the Theatre Royal with English and Irish words, for the pianoforte, violin or German flute [beginning: "How and how pleasing the birds sing in tune"], London, G. Walker (c.1820)

See Scholes *The Oxford Companion to Music*, tenth edition, for an entry on 'Robin Adair'.]

124. JACKSON'S MORNING BRUSH

TITLE: *1840, p.95:* Jackson's Morning Brush. Index, p.IV: Muisguilt Mhicseoin. Tune: *1840*, p.95.

NOTES

[Noted "from a piper in 1797". In the Index p.VIII, the composer is given as "Jackson, County Monaghan, in 1775". A detailed note on Jackson is in Groves *Dictionary of Music and Musicians*, Vol. IV (5th edition). There are also references to Jackson in the Introduction p.100 of the *1840* volume and in Flood's *History*, p.258/259. An authoritative article entitled 'Piper Jackson' is published by Breandán Breathnach in *Irish Folk Music Studies/Éigse Cheol Tíre*, Vol.2, pp.41-57. The following is a list of occurrences of the tune in other collections additional to those listed in the Breathnach article.

Aird's *Selection of Scotch, English and Irish Airs*, No.22 (c.1795)
O'Farrell's *Pocket Companion*, Vol. II, p.88 (1801-1810)
Holden's *Old Established Tunes*, Vol I, p.5 (1806-7)
Murphy's *Irish Airs and Jigs*, p.5 (1809)
O'Neill's *Irish Minstrels and Musicians*, p.135 (1913)
O'Neill's *Music of Ireland*, p.167 (1903)]

125. THE BONNY CUCKOO

TITLE: *1840, p.96:* The bonny cuckoo. Index p.I: An chuaichín mhaiseach. Tune: MS.33 bk.5, p.18. Marked "Andante Legato". One verse written over the words.

My bonny cuckoo, I tell you true,
That through the groves I'll rove with you;
I'll rove with you until the spring,
And then my cuckoo shall sweetly sing.
Cuckoo, sing girls, let no one tell,
Until I settle my seasons well.

The ash and the hazel shall mourning say,
My bonny cuckoo, don't go away;
Don't go away, but tarry here,
And make the season last all the year.
Don't go away, but tarry here,
And make the season last all the year.

NOTES

AIR: According to the Index the source is "Ballinascreen and from the late H. Joy. Esq. Belfast, 1793". Ballinascreen is in Co. Derry and Henry Joy was one of the founders of the United Irishmen. [In the Introduction p.95 Bunting writes: "From this ancient melody . . . another tune "The little and great mountain" (Sí beag, Sí mór) seems to have been arranged with some slight variations." It appears that O'Carolan used this tune as the basis of one of his songs entitled "Sí beag, Sí mor" which Bunting printed as No.63 in his *1796* collection.

The Carolan song is dealt with extensively in *DOSC* No.202. Other versions of 'the bonny cuckoo' are to be found in Neale's *Celebrated Irish Tunes* (c.1726), p.14, "Cuckoo"; and Mulholland's *Ancient Irish Airs* (1810), p.59. The tune also occurs on page I of the introduction to the *1840* volume.]

WORDS: Probably from Henry Joy. Bunting's Irish title is a mistranslation.

126. FEADGHAIL AN AIRIMH (CONNDAE AN RIGH)
Ploughman's Whistle, King's County

TITLE: *1840, p.96:* Ploughman's Whistle (Queen's County). Index, p.iv: Feaduidhil an airimh, Condae an Righ. The Ploughman's Whistle, King's County; p.ix: Ploughman's Whistle, Queen's County. Tune: MS.12, I "Plough Whistle. King's County." The key signature of four flats is here corrected to three flats.

NOTES

Bunting seems to have been in a state of muddle over the provenance of this tune. It will be seen that in the title over the music and in the English Index he gives its origin as the Queen's County and in the Irish Index he gives it as the King's County. But the matter is worse than that. Bunting published two tunes entitled "Ploughman's Whistle" — Nos. 126 and 137. In the Index it is stated, correctly, that No.126 was obtained from Petrie and No.137 from Charles Byrne the harper. Yet in the Introduction, p.96, his comment on No.126 (Petrie's air) is that "this curious melody is given in Walker's Irish Bards" — which is not the case; and he gives the title "Ploughman's Whistle of the King's County" to No.137 without mentioning the name of the contributor. There is in Walker, Vol.I, at end No.xiii, a piece entitled "Plough Tune", which is a variant of No.137 in the *1840* volume. In the Introduction (p.96), Bunting states that "the tune must be played very slowly and with the utmost expression".

Bunting's errors, however, had the great advantage of inducing Petrie to deal with the subject of the Ploughman's Whistle at considerable length in his scholarly *Ancient Music of Ireland* (1855). Five of the large quarto pages are devoted to the subject (pp.26-29). He refutes Bunting without rancour, prints his own King's County tune as noted by him in 1821, and adds two others: one from Mr. James Fogarty of Tibroghney, County Kilkenny and the other (also noted by himself) from the whistling of Teige MacMahon, a County Clare peasant whose name appears so frequently in Stanford's edition of the Petrie MSS. MacMahon's words were also given by Petrie in the original Irish, with an English translation by his friend the noted scholar Eugene O'Curry, who was a native of Clare.

[In MS.12, I, there is another piece entitled "Ploughman's Whistle, King's County". It is in the form of rough sketches.]

TURLOGH O'CAROLAN

DENIS HEMPSON

127. TOBIAS PEYTON

TITLE: *1840, p.97:* Toby Peyton's Plangsty. Index, p.V: Planxtae Teaboid Peiton. Tune: *Forde MS.*, p.298.

NOTES

Noted from Hugh Higgins, Harper in 1792 (Index, p.IX).

Of the several versions of this tune by Carolan I have chosen one from the *Forde MSS.* because it appears to be the most authentic. It is printed in my edition of Carolan, Vol.I, No.148, with notes in Vol.II, pp.92-94. Forde points out two mistakes in Bunting's version.

On page 99 of the Introduction of the *1840* volume, Bunting has the following note:

"Squire Toby Peyton, of Lisduff, in the county of Leitrim, was an Irish gentleman of the old school, a sportsman, convivialist, and an ardent lover of the harp. O'Neill (the harper), in whose time he was still living and who often enjoyed the hospitalities of Lisduff, gives this account of him: 'Toby Peyton had a fine unencumbered estate, and, exclusive of the expenses of groceries and spices, spent the remainder of his income in encouraging national diversions,

185

particularly harping and playing on all other stringed instruments. He lived to the age of 104 years, and when he was 100 would mount his horse as active as a man of twenty, and be the first in at the death, whether it was a fox or a hare.' The tune had its origin in the following circumstance. The squire, meeting Carolan on horseback, said to him jocosely in Irish, 'Carolan, you ride crooked', to which the harper, who was exceedingly sensitive in every thing touching his personal appearance, replied, 'I'll pay you for that with a crooked tune'. He accordingly composed this air, which is in truth of such a crabbed, unmanageable nature as almost to defy every rule of composition in the adaptation of a bass."

In Ó Máille's edition of Carolan's poems (1916), p.134, there are three quatrains headed in the MS. "Planxty Peyton" — Planxty being a term often prefixed by Carolan to the surname of a lively melody for one of his patrons. These laudatory verses are presumably intended for the tune; but they are extremely poor and are not worth printing and translating.

According to the records in the Office of Arms, Toby Peyton died in August, 1768. Probably he is buried in Fenagh Churchyard, close to his home. A tombstone there bears the inscription "Here lyes the Peytons and their wives"

128. THE COUNTY TYRONE

TITLE: *1840, p.97:* The County Tyrone. Index, p.III: Contae Thír Eoghain.
Tune: MS.33, bk.6, p.2: "This is the gen. . . new . . . oyne edition".

NOTES

[The Index p.X gives the source as "J. McCracken Esq. Belfast. 1800".

The key signature of the MS version above has been changed from three to two sharps, since G natural was written throughout. Likewise, the note *B* is constantly flat throughout the *1840* version of the tune.]

129. AN MAIDRÍN RUA
The Little Fox

TITLE: *1840, p.98:* The Little bold fox. Index p.II: An maidrín ruadh. Tune: *1840*, p.98.

NOTES

[The source given in the Index p.XI is "G. Petrie Esq., Dublin. 1839". Other versions of the tune including the appropriate verses, are to be found in *Londubh an Chairn* (Hannagan), No.28, and in *Ceol* [*Ár Sinsear* (Walsh), p.41. Bunting version needs an eight line verse, and the chorus as marked by him needs to be repeated if the usual four line chorus is to fit it.]

187

130. AN CRÚISGÍN BEAG
The Little Jug

TITLE: *1840, p.98:* The Little Pot. Index p.I: An crúisgín bheag. Tune: *1840,* p.98.

NOTES

[Noted from "Miss Murphy, Dublin, 1839." This tune is probably a variant of "An Crúiscín Lán" which is still sung today in West Cork and the words of which fit the Bunting tune. The earliest vesion is to be found in an 18th Century English Ballad Opera called *The Beggar's Wedding* written by Charles Coffey, an Irishman. This was performed in 1728.

Five verses and a translation, including four verses of a second version, are to be found in O Daly's *Poets and Poetry of Munster,* p.162, with the title "An Crúisgín Lán".]

131. THE HURLER'S MARCH

TITLE: *1840, p.99:* The Hurler's March (King's County). Index p.VI: Triall an Iománaigh. Tune: MS.33 bk.4, p.42 — no key signature.

NOTES

[In the Index p.XI the source given is "G. Petrie Esq. Dublin. 1839". The printed version is pentatonic while the MS. version (above) is heptatonic. The latter has no key signature in the MS.

Tune No. 990 in *Stanford Petrie* is entitled "The Hurler's March" but bears little resemblance to Bunting's tune beyond the fact that it is in double jig rhythm.

A copy of the tune in MS.12, I is identical to the published version.

There is a double jig in vogue to-day, with the title The Hurler's March, which has little or no relationship with Bunting's tune. Versions will be found in Breandán Breathnach's *Ceol Rince na hÉireann* (tune No.31), and in Pat Mitchell's *The Dance Music of Willy Clancy* (No.145).]

132. BLÁTH DONN IS BÁN
The brown and white blossom

TITLE: *1840, p.99:* The brown and white garland. Index, p.II: Blath donn is bán. Tune: *1840*, p.99.

NOTES

There are no words for this tune, which was obtained from George

Petrie in 1839. On page 98 of his Introduction, Bunting states that it "is allied to that peculiar class of airs called *Lunigs* in Scotland and *Lobeens* in Ireland, of which three other specimens are noticed below [Nos. 134, 135 and 136]. It has been a favourite at the festive meetings of the peasantry from time immemorial. It is first sung by one person and then repeated in chorus by the whole assembly. The setting given here, which is that of the air as popularly sung, seems irregular in the transposition of the first four bars, which ought to occupy the place of the second four, and *vice versa*, to make the arrangement correspond with the model on which Irish melodies are generally constructed".

133. DÁ MBEADH CÚIRT AGAM IS CAISLEÁN
If I had a court and castle

TITLE: *1840, p.99:* If I had a court and castle. Index, p.III: Da mbeidh cuirt agam is caislean. Tune: *1840*, No.133.

WORDS: MS. 7, No.124

Go Cúige Uladh má théann tú, 'do dhéidh-se ní bheidh mé beó,
Agus Cúige Chonnacht ní thréigfidh mé go dtéighe mé faoi fhód.
A ógánaigh bhinn bhréagaigh, is in do bhéilín do gheobhainn cluain,
Nachar tharraing tú an uile léan orm, 's gud chuige a n-éalófá uaim?

190

Ba mhór an díobhail eolais do bhuachaill óg a bheith 'mo dhéidh,
'S go bhfuil mé faoi mo mhóide ag aon óigfhear le bliain;
Ní phósfaidh mé stróinse nó seanduine críon liath,
'S do shiúlfainn an domhan mór leat-sa, a stóirín, is déanam réidh!

Dá mbeadh cúirt agam a's caisleán, ní bheadh seachrán ar mo ghrádh,
Bheadh ór buidhe in a phóca aige agus airgead bán;
Níor mhór liom an uile shórt duit d'fhóirfeadh ar mhac an righe —
Agus fill abhaile, a stóirín, agus tóg an dólás de mo chroidhe!

Is faide liom ná fios (?) mo shaoighil go bhfuil an oidhche ag druidint liom,
Ag súil go bhfeicfinn rún mo chroidhe, mar is leis ba mhian liom bheith ag caint.
Is é nár dhubhairt ariamh liom: "Fág mo shlighe a's ná bí ann!"
Ach go deó mo chuid den tsaoghal thú — tóg do chroidhe 's ná caill do ghreann!

TRANSLATION

1. If you go to Ulster, I shall not remain alive in your absence, And I shall not leave Connacht until I go under the sod. Lovely but false young man, 'tis in your mouth I'd get flattery, Did you not bring every grief to me, and why will you leave me? 2. It is great folly for a young lad to pursue me, When I am engaged to another young man for a year. I shall never marry a stranger nor a withered, grey old man, And I would walk the great world with you, and let us agree! 3. If I had a court and a castle, my loved one would not stray, He would have yellow gold in his pocket and white silver; I would not care for someone else, fit to be the son of a king — And come back, my dearest, and relieve my heart of its sorrow. 4. It seems longer to me than a lifetime until evening comes, Hoping to see my heart's love, for it is to him I'd love to talk He never said to me, "Leave my way and don't be there!" But 'tis you are for ever my share of the world — lift up your heart and don't lose your affection!

NOTES

AIR: Obtained from Miss Murphy, Dublin, in 1839. Bunting's title is the beginning of the third verse.

I have found no other version of this air or words. The tune is irregular with eight bars in the first section and twelve in the second part. Consequently the words to not fit the tune. Also in the *1840* volume, the tune is marked "Moderately Quick and Chearful" [sic], which the words certainly are not. There are three more verses in the MS but I have omitted them because they are muddled and do not make sense.

134. LÚIBÍN
Spinning Wheel Song

TITLE: *1840, p.100:* The spinning wheel song. Index, p.II: An Luibín. Tune: *1840*, p.100: An lúibín — The spinning wheel song.

NOTES

This is the first of three spinning wheel songs received by Bunting from Miss Murphy of Dublin in 1839. Unfortunately no words have been found for them in the Bunting MSS.

He states in his Introduction, pp. 98/99: "The loobeen (lúibín) is a peculiar species of chaunt, having a very well marked time, and a frequently recurring chorus or catchword. It is sung at the merry-makings and assemblages of the young women when they meet at 'spinnings' or 'quiltings' and is accompanied by extraneous verses, of which each singer furnishes a line. The intervention of the chorus after each line gives time for the preparation of the succeeding one by the next singer, and thus the Loobeen goes round until the chain of song is completed. Hence its name, signifying literally the 'link' tune. Of course there is a great variety of words, and these are usually of a ludicrous character, such as might be expected from the 'crambo' of rustics."

The other two songs are Nos. 135 and 136. But see also No. 132 and the note thereto.

[All three tunes are in 6/8 time and an analysis of the form of each brings out certain common characteristics: No. 134 consists of one 6 bar phrase; No. 135 can be subdivided into a 6 bar phrase and a 4 bar phrase, and No. 136 falls into an 4 bar phrase and a 6 bar phrase.

The 6 bar phrase is therefore common to all three tunes. Also the note D flat is consistent throughout Nos. 134 and 135 and have been included here in the key signature. Note that the three tunes are hexatonic with the notes A, F and G, respectively, missing.

Of the Petrie tunes (see below), Nos. 1366 (with its variant No. 1474) and 1475 consist of single six-bar phrases. William Forde on p.170 of his MSS refers to 'Brighid Na bPéarlaí' (Bunting *1809 Collection*, p.72) also as a spinning-wheel song.]

Three women's occupation songs (airs and Irish words) were published by Mrs. E. Costello in her *"Amhráin Mhuighe Seola"*, pp. 93-96, issued as Vol. XVI of the *Journal of the Irish Folk Song Society* (1919). They were probably spinning songs. I printed another from Donegal, with Irish words, in Vol. XVII of the *Journal* (1920) p.13.

The following spinning tunes, all of them from County Clare, are in Stanford's edition of the Petrie MSS. Nos. 1366, 1367, 1368, 1369, 1473, 1474, 1475.

135. LÚIBÍN
Spinning Wheel Song

TITLE: *1840, p.100:* The spinning wheel song. Index, p.II: An Lúibín. Tune: *1840*, p.100: An luibin — The spinning wheel song.

NOTES
[This tune like No.134 is hexatonic with the note F missing. Also the note D flat is consistent throughout and is included in the key signature above.

See note to No. 134.]

136. LÚIBÍN
Spinning wheel song

TITLE: *1840, p.100:* The spinning wheel song. Index, p.II: An Luibín. Tune: MS.12, I "Looben, the young man's song in answer to the womens' "

NOTES

[As in the case of the previous two tunes this tune is hexatonic with the note G missing. See notes to No. 134.

In the MS. Bunting writes under the tune: "These last three tunes with extempore verses made for the occasion are sung in the order of arrangement as here given by the women at their merry spinning wheel or campines (?). The verses between the young women and men sometimes extended in duration for hours comprehended all their innocent joyous thoughts".]

137. FEADGHAIL AN AIRIMH
The Ploughman's Whistle

TITLE: *1840, p.101:* Ploughman's whistle. Index, p.IV: Feaduidhil an Airimh. Tune: MS. 12(2).

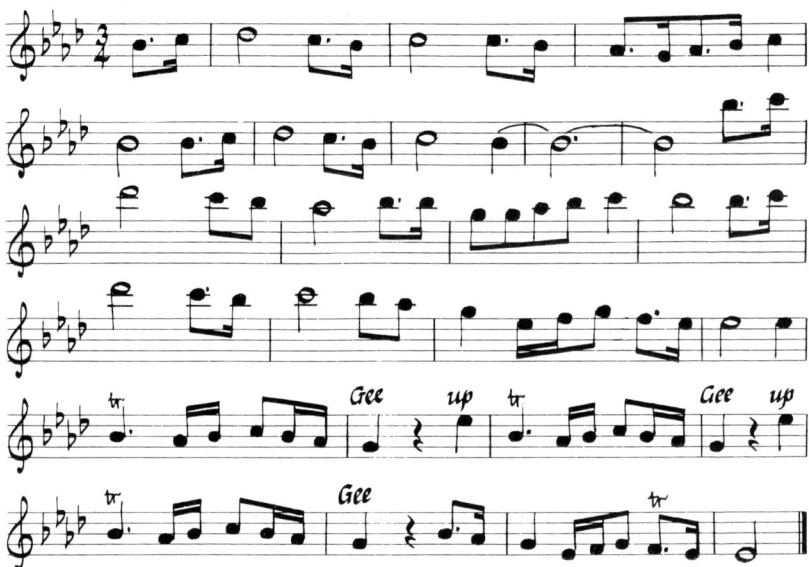

NOTES
[Noted from "Byrne, harper, in 1803".

The note D flat is consistent throughout the MS. version and the key signature has been corrected to four flats above. See also No. 126, this edition. A variant is to be found in Walker's *Irish Bards*, No. XIII at the end.]

138. INÍON AN TOICE AGUS AN MAIRNÉALACH
The Wenches Daughter and the Sailor

TITLE: *1840, p.102:* A Sailor loved a Farmer's Daughter. Index, p.IV: Inghean an toicigh agus an Mairnealach. A sailor and a Farmer's Daughter. Tune: *1840,* p.102.

NOTES
[The index gives the source as "G. Petrie, Esq. Dublin, 1839". Bunting's title is an incorrect translation of the Irish title given on p.IV of the Index. The Bunting tune is reproduced in Stanford's *Songs of Old Ireland*, p.83 with new words by Alfred Perceval Graves entitled 'A Sailor Lad wooed a Farmer's Daughter".]

139. MAEBH GHEAL

TITLE: *1840, p.102:* O! White Maive. Index, p.V: Ó! Maebhi gheal Ó! Tune: MS. 5, p.14. "Meibhe gheall o, o ri!" Similar copies in MS.5 pp.32 and 37 with similar titles.

NOTES

[Noted from "Kitty Doo, at Armagh. 1780" (?). In printing the tune, Bunting altered it in several ways. Firstly, he changed what was a hexatonic tune (see MS. version) into an heptatonic tune by including some passing notes (bars 7 and 11) and adding another flat to the key signature. Secondly he changed the form of the piece from A A¹ A¹ B to A A¹ A¹ A². Thirdly, he substituted the first phrase for the final phrase, presumably in order to give a symmetrical number of bars in each phrase.]

140. AN BROMACH FÍADHAIN
The wild colt

TITLE: *1840, p.103:* The wild colt. Index, p.II: An bromach fiadhain. Tune: *1840*, p.103.

196

NOTES

This tune was contributed by George Petrie in 1839. Though there are no extant words, there can be little doubt that the English title is the correct one and the Irish title a translation.

[The rhythm is that of a slip jig. In the *1840* volume Bunting repeats the tune once with a different bass. The basic sixteen-bar tune is given above.]

141. TÁ MÉ I n-ÉAGMAIS ACH ÍOCFADH MÉ FÓS
I'm in debt but I'll pay them yet

TITLE: *1840, p.103:* I will pay them yet. Index, p.VI: Ta me a neug-mhais ac iochfaidm mhe fas — I'm in debt, but I'll pay them yet. Tune: MS. 5, p.33: "Disapated Youth." "Stannish an Arrish." "I'm in debt but I'll pay them yet".

NOTES

Taken down by Bunting from "Mrs. B." at Oranmore, Co. Galway in 1839". This is a song-air, but I have found no words for it, either in the Bunting MSS. or elsewhere.

In his *1855 volume*, pp. 107-109, Petrie prints a version of the tune, entitled "The Monks of the Screw". He explains that this was the mock title of a "Singular social union of wit and talent which existed in Dublin from the year 1779 to the close of the year 1785". Its "Prior" was the noted lawyer John Philpot Curran, who wrote the song ["The monks of the screw"] to a tune "which, no doubt, he had learnt in his own loved county of Cork". Curran's daughter Sarah was engaged to be married to Robert Emmet, one of the leaders of the rising of 1798, who was captured hanged and beheaded.

[In the MS. Bunting writes "Disapated Youth" which is the name of a tune in his *1796* collection (see *DOSB* I p.26 et seq.) but there is no connection between the two tunes.

The song "Táim in Arrears" is a variant of Bunting's tune. It can be found, words and tune, in *Londubh an Chairn* (Hannagan), No. 56 with another version in *Amhráin Muighe Sheóla* (Costello). The words are also to be found in O'Daly's *Miscellany*. Another version of the tune is to be found in the journal *Ceol*, Volume 2, No. 4, where we are informed that 'Moll Roe' is a common name for the tune. It is found, under the latter title, in O'Neill's *Dance Music of Ireland* (No.441).]

142. A LOVELY NUN TO A FRIAR CAME

TITLE: *1840, p.104:* A Lovely Lass to a Friar Came. Index, p.II: Cailin Deas Chum Brathar Tainic. Tune: MS.29, p.44: "Friar and Nun." A very rough copy. No key or time signature.

A lovely nun to a friar came
  To confess in a morning early.
"In what, my dear, are you to blame?
  Come, tell me most sincerely."
"Alas, my guilt I dare not name,
  But my lad he loved me dearly."

NOTES

The copy on which Bunting has based the printed version along with the words (one verse only) is in MS.12, bk.2, p.30, with the following note: "This air is given on Hempson's authority as being an Irish melody. He had learned it from his first master; but many other harpers had it and played it with the same variation of the octave to imitate the soft effeminate acute tone of the young nun and the masculine deep voice of the friar at confession." The word "nun" is struck out and the word "lass" substituted.

The tune is repeated in the same MS. on p.35, with the title "A lovely lass to a friar came". The note on it reads: "This was a favourite tune with the old harpers and listened to by every auditor with great delight. It is supposed to be descriptive of the conversation between a friar and a young woman at confession, and the tune in the higher octave is intended as an imitation of her voice, the lower tones that of the friar. The harpers universally believed it to be Irish, from two circumstances: the range of the melody being confined to six notes and the shortness of the phrases. The four notes in the first bar sound so like what is met with in all the older airs that we can hardly doubt its identity as an Irish melody. It has been played times out of mind in this Kingdom as an Irish Melody."

[The Index gives the source as "Hempson, at Magilligan, 1796," and at the head of the piece on p.104 we find "The Var: by Lyons in 1698". On p.100 of the Introduction to the *1840* volume Bunting writes:

"This is the only air admitted into the collection which is not of unquestionable Irish origin; but the editor has adopted it as Irish, on the authority of all the old harpers with whom he has conversed: it was at all times a favourite tune of theirs. The emphatic manner in which the fourth tone of the scale is used, seems to claim for it a high antiquity, and justifies the restoration of the air to its proper place among the melodies of Ireland. It is a very sweet tune, and the higher and lower octaves aptly coincide with the alternations of the male and female voices in the song."

In *The British Broadside Ballad and its Music* (New Jersey, 1966), C.M. Simpson deals with two distinct tunes under the title "The Fryar and the Nun". The earliest reference to a variant of the Bunting tune is in an engraved single-sheet edition, conjecturally dated 1710, in the British Museum.]

143. FAIRE! FAIRE! AR AGHAIDH! AR AGHAIDH!
Watch! Watch! Forward! Forward!

TITLE: *1840, p.105:* The Pharroh or War March. Index, p.III: Faire! Faire! Ar aghaidh ar aghaidh. Tune: MS.33, bk.4, p.56: "Yellow Wattle 2nd set". [Bunting's omission of the seventh bar of the second section has been corrected here.]

NOTES

This tune, for which there are no words, was obtained from George Petrie in 1835.

[As printed it consists of nine sections, the last three of which were probably added by Bunting.

A variant is printed in Breandán Breathnach's *Ceol Rince na hÉireann*, No.12, 'Port Liatroma'. A list of the occurrences of the tune elsewhere is to be found in the notes on p.88 of the same book.

The tune printed above, entitled "Yellow Wattle 2nd Set", is a variant of Bunting's printed tune. On the previous page in the MS. is "Yellow Wattle, 1st Set".]

144. TUIREAMH UÍ RAGHALLAIGH
Lament for O'Reilly

TITLE: *1840, p.106:* Tuireamh Uí Raghallaigh — O'Reilly's Lament. Index, p.VI: Tuireamh Ui Raghalliagh. Tune: MS.34/30.

WORDS: MS.34/30

> The fate of the battle is past
> O'Reilly stood firm to the last
> His friends round him lay
> Yet he still kept the day
> Till he fell to the ground
> There his bosom all gored
> And still grasping his sword
> O'Reilly was found.

NOTES

MS. 34/30 consists of four sheets. The first two give the version of the tune printed above, followed by the same tune transposed to the key of C, which makes it unsingable. There is the following note beneath the music:

"After a sanguinary conflict in which this hero had the misfortune of beholding all who could bear arms of his dear kindred and followers fall by his side, he, though alone, had the glory of impeding for a time the progress of the enemy, maintaining by the prowess of his single arm the pass at Finea — 'till at length being "weary with extreme toil" and sick at heart from sad forebodings of his country's ruin, he fell — but not alone. The "Emerald of Europe" fell with him."

The title, placed above the music is: "Erin's lament for the loss of O'Reilly, surnamed "MYLES THE SLASHER" from his amazing bodily strength and undaunted courage."

On sheet 2 are the following words, evidently intended to serve as the conclusion of the above note:

"Near the spot where his remains were found, covered with wounds but still grasping his sword, sad Erin has taught (?) a rude rock thus to express her feeling:

Traveller!
Weep not O'Reilly's
but his
Country's loss!''

Sheets 3 and 4 give the words (five verses) of which Verse IV is given above. Bunting has the following annotation on p.92 of his Introduction: "The O'Reilly, in commemoration of whom this melody was arranged, was Maolmordha or Miles, surnamed 'The Slasher', probably the son of Maolmordha Dha (Deas), or Miles 'the handsome', who was 'The Queen's O'Reilly' in the reign of Elizabeth. Miles the Slasher was colonel of horse in the army commanded by Lord Castlehaven in the wars which followed the rebellion of 1641, and was slain valiantly defending the bridge of Finea against Monro's Scotch in 1644. (See Castlehaven's *Memoirs*)".

The tune was given to Bunting by J. O'Reilly, Esq., Belfast, in 1806. In the *1840* volume Bunting printed the tune in 3/4 time instead of 4/4 time as in the MS. version.

145. ACHILL AIR

TITLE: *1840, p.106:* Achil Air. Index, p.IV: Fonn Aichle. Tune: *1840,* p.106.

NOTES

This tune was given to Bunting by George Petrie in 1839. Achill is an island off the coast of Co. Mayo. The name of the singer is not known, and there are no extant words. [The notes A flat and D flat are consistent throughout the tune with the exception of an A natural in bar 11. The key signature should, therefore, be four flats as corrected above.]

146. GEARRFHIADH 'SAN ARBHAR
The Hare in the Corn

TITLE: *1840, p.107:* The Hare in the Corn. Index, p.IV: Gearrfhiadh San nArbhar. Tune: *1840*, p.107.

NOTES

Bunting has the following comment on p.98 of his Introduction: "An ancient tune for the pipes, in which there is an imitation of a hunt, including the sound of the huntsmen's horns, the crying of the dogs, and finally the distress and death of the hare. This performance can only be given on the pipes, the chanter or principal tube of which, when pressed with its lower end against the leather guard on the performer's knee, can be made to yield a smothered, sobbing tone, very appropriate to the dying cry of the hare, but difficult to imitate or describe in musical notation." ·

The air was noted in 1800 from a piper whose name is not given.

[The tune also appears in the following collections:
Kinlock's *100 Airs* No.48
O'Neill's *Music of Ireland*, p.143
McFadden's *Scotch, English, Irish and Foreign Airs*, Volume V, p.25
O'Farrell's *Pocket Companion for the Union Pipes*, Vol. 1, p.77
Wright's *Compleat Collection of Celebrated Country Dances*, Vol. I, p.4
Holden's *Most Esteemed Irish Melodies*, Vol. II, No.35
O'Neill's *Dance Music of Ireland*, No.49 and No.254 ("The Absent-Minded Man")]

147. THE CHANTER'S TUNE

TITLE: *1840, p.107:* The chanter's tune. Index, p.X: Fonn an Abhranaidh. Tune: *1840*, p.107.

Given to Bunting by "E. Shannon, Esq.", in 1839. There is no MS. version, and no words have been found.

[The note E flat is consistent throughout the tune and has been included in the key signature above. The title indicates that this tune is probably a piper's piece, as is the case with the previous tune (No. 146).]

148. IS FADA ANNSO MÉ or THE GENTLE MAIDEN
I am a long time here

TITLE: *1840, p.108:* Long am I here, or the gentle maiden. Index, p.II: As fada annso mé. Tune: *1840*, p.108.

NOTES
It will be observed that Bunting gives two titles for this tune, one Irish and the other English. These appear only in the English Index, from which we learn that it was obtained from Miss Murphy of Dublin in 1839. On a small detached sheet in the middle of Bunting MS. 12, bk. I is written "I am a long time here", which suggests that the appropriate words are Irish.

[In MS. 5, p.52 there is a tune which is a variant of "The Gentle Maiden" with the title "The Bare-Headed Poor Old Man". This also appears in MS.12, bk.I.

205

Another variant under the title "It is my deep sorrow" is given with notes, in the *Journal of the Irish Folk Song Society*, Vol. X, p.10 and yet another, entitled "Owen Coir", is in the same journal Vol. X, p.21.]

149. KILKENNY TUNE

TITLE: *1840, p.108:* Kilkenny tune. Index, p.IV: Fonn Cille Camnigh. Tune: *1840*, p.108.

NOTES
Noted from E. Shannon Esq., Dublin in 1839. [The note A flat is consistent throughout and has been included in the key signature above.]

150. THE FOGGY DEW

TITLE: *1840, p.109:* The Foggy Dew. Index, p.III: Drucht an cheo. Tune: *1840*, p.109.

NOTES

Noted from "J. McKnight, Esq., Belfast 1839". [In Bars 10, 11, 18, 19, Bunting includes an E natural presumably for harmonic reasons and the E flat has been retained in the version printed above. This tune is a variant of "Sloan's Lamentation", No.117 in this edition, and is also to be found in the *Journal of the Irish Folk Song Society*, Vol. III, p.33.

Variants also appear in O'Neill's *Music of Ireland*, p.33 and in Joyce's *Old Irish Folk Music and Song*, p.31, where the tune is compared with "Ar thaobh na carraige báine" in Petrie's *Ancient Music of Ireland*, p.143. (cf. No.26 this edition).

A song under the same title as Bunting's is in *Traditional Tunes* by Frank Kidson, (Oxford, 1891). Margaret Dean-Smith in *A Guide to English Folk Song Collections* p.67, remarks on the Kidson song thus: "The air, taken from a MS. dated c.1825 is of the same structure as that in Sharp's *English Folk Carols* (1911) but the melody is different from that usually asociated with the English version of the song and nearer to that noted by Bunting."]

151. IRISH JIG

TITLE: *1840, p.109:* Irish jig. Index, p.V: Rainnce Gaodhalach. Tune: *1840*, p.109.

NOTES

This is a typical double jig, with two parts of eight bars in 6/8 time. It was noted from Macauley of Ballymoney, County Antrim in 1793.

APPENDIX I

[Apart from the tunes published in the main body of the *1840* volume, Bunting also published seven tunes in Chapter I, and a supplement of eight tunes in Chapter VI of the Introduction. Ten of these are taken from various parts of Bunting's three collections and have been dealt with in the appropriate part of *DOSB*.
The remaining five tunes are dealt with in this appendix.]

152. FADA AN LÁ GAN CLANN UISNEACH
Long is the day without the Sons of Uisneach

TITLE: *1840, Intro. facing p.88:* The Lamentation of Deirdre for Sons of Usneach. Tune: MS.5, p.42: "Song of Clan Uisneach in the Poem of Deirdre".

Fada an lá gan clann Uisneach
Níor thuirseach bheith 'na gcuallacht,
Mic ríogh re a ndíoltaí deoraidh,
Trí leomhain Chnuic na nUamha.

Trí leannáin do mhnáibh Breatan,
Trí seabhaic Sléibhe Cuillin,
Mic ríogh dár ghéill an gaisge
's dá dtugdís amhais uirrim.

Na trí beithreacha beodha
Trí leomhain Leasa Connrach
Mic ríogh nár mhian a moladh,
Trí mic ochta na nOlltach.

TRANSLATION

1. Long is the day without the sons of Uisneach, It was not wearisome to be in their company, A King's sons by whom exiles were supported (?) Three lions of Cnoc na nUamha. 2. Three beloved of the women of Britain, Three hawks of Sliabh Cuillinn, A King's sons to whom warriors yielded, And to whom mercenaries gave honour. 3. Three valiant bears, Three lions of Lios Connrach, Chiefs who did not seek praise, Three sons beloved of the men of Ulster.

NOTES

AIR: [The copy on which Bunting based the published arrangement is in MS. 27, p.60. The tune in MS.5, p.42 (edited above) has an unnecessary F sharp in the key signature since it is a hexatonic tune with the note 'F' missing. On page 83 *et seq.* of the Introduction, Bunting writes in detail about the background to the song. We learn from a letter to Bunting from Dr. James MacDonnell in 1839 that Bunting obtained two versions of the piece, one in Murloch, Co. Antrim and the other from "the old Marchioness of Londonderry" who learned it from a "Blind Highland Woman". The tune is printed with some notes in Vol. VIII of the *Journal of the Irish Folk Song Society* under the title "A Song of the Antrim Glens and Scottish Isles". It is also to be found in the Bunting MSS. in MS.13, p.27; MS.12, I and MS.5, p.46.

WORDS: The first three of eighteen verses in *Dunaire Gaedhlge*, Vol. III, p.83, by Róis Ní Ógáin are given above. A translation is given on p.165 of the same volume. The poem is also edited in *Seacht Sár-Dhánta Gaedhilge* by Tomás Ó Flannghaile.]

153. CAIDÉ SIN DO'N TÉ SIN NACH mBAINEANN SIN DÓ
What is that to him whom it does not concern

TITLE: *1840, Intro. p.15:* Go de sin den te sin; what is that to him. Tune: MS.33, bk.2, p.55 — "Tune No.100." "From Denis Hempson".

NOTES

[Five verses of a song under the same title may be found on p.239 of *Dhá Chéad de Cheoltaibh Uladh* by Enrí Ó Muirgheasa. On p.453 of the same volume, the appropriate tune is given in tonic Sol-fa, but apart from a similar time signature it does not resemble Bunting's tune.

Bunting uses this piece in the Introduction as an example of a pentatonic tune. The MS. version, however, is hexatonic.]

154. OSSIANIC AIR

TITLE: *1840, Intro. supplement p.3:* Ossianic Air — sung in the Highlands of Scotland. Tune: MS.12, bk.2.

NOTES

[Bunting obtained this tune from Sir John Sinclair of Edinburgh, who wrote to him in 1808, explaining that it was "recently transmitted to me by the Rev. Mr. Cameron, Minister of Halkirk, in the county of Caithness, North Britain, who learned it many years ago from a very old man, a farmer on my estate, who was accustomed to sing some of Ossian's poems to that air with infinite delight and enthusiasm".

Although the MS. and published version differ rhythmically, they are identical melodically. Both are hexatonic tunes, with the note 'F' missing in the MS. version.]

155. ARGAN MÓR

TITLE: *1840, Intro, supplement, p.3:* The Battle of Argan More. Intro. p.88: Argan Mor. Tune: MS.12, I.

NOTES

[The tune occurs twice in the Bunting MSS: MS. 12, I — given above. This is obviously Bunting's original sketch and one verse of the words is written beneath the notes. MS. 27, p.59 — also has the words beneath the notes. This is the fair copy of the published arrangement. A note underneath the piece reads: "written down from a Cushendall man in 1809 tenant to Dr. McDonnell". The tune is pentatonic with the notes 'B' and 'E' missing.]

156. FAIGH AN GLÉAS
Find the Key

TITLE: *1840, Intro., p.I of supplement:* Feagh an Geleash or Try if it is in tune. Tune: MS. 29, p.50, 51.

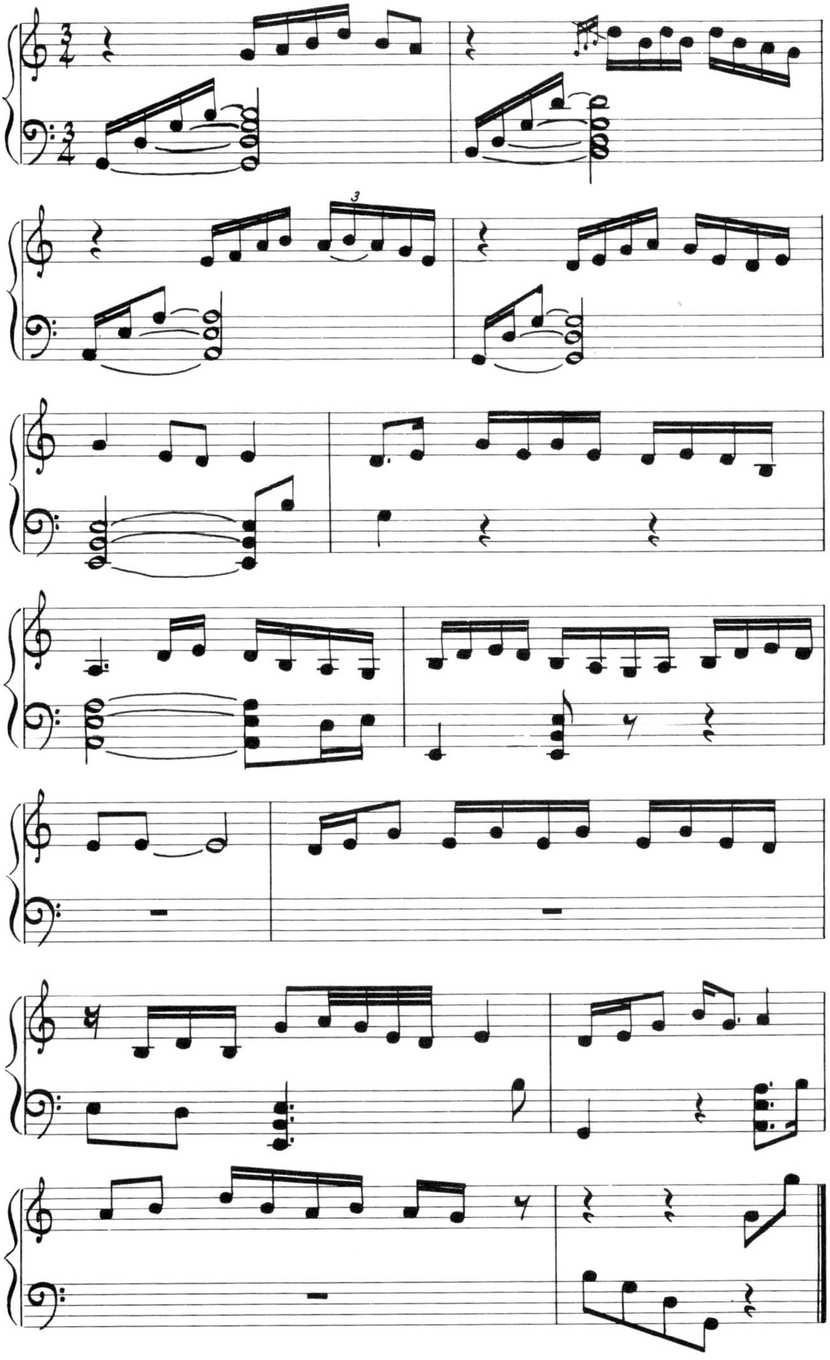
3

NOTES

[In a note on p.82 of the Introduction, Bunting describes the piece as "an ancient Irish prelude" and states that it was obtained from Hempson in 1792. "It was with great reluctance that the old harper was prevailed on to play even the fragment of it here preserved, to gratify the Editor, to whom he acknowledged he was under obligations. He would rather, he asserted, have played any other air, as this awakened recollections of the days of his youth, of friends whom he had outlived, and of times long past, when the harpers were accustomed to play the ancient caoinans or lamenations, with their corresponding preludes. When pressed to play, notwithstanding, his peevish answer uniformly was, "What's the use of doing so? no one can understand it now, not even any of the harpers now living." The piece occurs six times in the MSS.

1. MS.29, p.48/49: "Veaghan Gleash" − a very rough effort at notating the tune. This is obviously Bunting's original sketch of Hempson's performance.

2. MS. 29, p.50, 51: This occurrence of the piece immediately follows the one just mentioned above, and is an effort to introduce bar lines and to stabilise the rhythm. This is a rough copy and many of the notes are difficult to decipher. It is edited above.

3. MS.27, on some loose pages at the end:− very close to the published version.

4. MS.33, bk.2, p.55: close to the published version.

5. MS.12, bk.I: a fair copy of the published version.

6. MS.12, bk.II: a second fair copy.

An interesting point to note in MS.29, p.48/49 is that all the chords omit the 3rd with the exception of the second and final chords. In MS.29, p.50, 51, Bunting includes the third in the first chord also. When it came to publishing the tune he included a 3rd in two more chords.

A footnote on p.83 of the Introduction states that the upward arpeggios in the piece are a printer's error and that they should be downward arpeggios "according to the practice of the ancient Irish harpers". The various MS. versions, with the exception of the fair copies, do not bear this out, however, since they all include upward arpeggios. The treble of the published version is pentatonic, while the bass is hexatonic on account of the added thirds already mentioned. The MS. version is entirely pentatonic with the exception of one 'F' in Bar 3. There is no key signature in the MS. version given above.]

APPENDIX II

NOTES AND SUGGESTED EMENDATIONS TO THE SONG TEXTS IN THIS EDITION

Number
7. Trans. I:1. For *woodlark* read *hen blackbird*.
11. Text I:2 Grammatically doubtful. Text and trans. of II:1 are obscure and trans. is doubtful.
13. Text I:6 for *léigheadh* read *léigeadh*. Trans. of this line is more than likely as follows: "Who used give the longest credit in the matter of payment of rent."
16. Text I:3 *Thrí an lasadh* is doubtful. Trans. II:3, for *lively* read *destitute*. Trans. II:7 (a person) who would send me back home without even my shoes. The last four lines of II of text and trans. are doubtful.
17. Text III.4, for *ar chlumha* read *ar chlúmh*.
    Text VII:3, the form *tuisleóga* is doubtful.
    Text VIII:3, the form *luaighi* is doubtful.
18. Second last two lines of text are doubtful.
19. Text VI:1, for *dár bhú liom* read *dar bha liom* as a possibility.
    VIII:3, for *claonadh* read *claonta* as a possibility.
25. Trans. I, for *from the north* read *to the north*.
27. Text I:7, for *léigheann* read *léighinn*.
29. Text IV:4, for *a béal* read *a béil*.
32. Text II:6, *a chéad* is doubtful.
46. Trans. III:4, for *to those pastures of Granuaile* read *from the treacherous one for Granuaile*.
    Trans. IV:4, *her elegiac music will be pleasant in the ears of Grainne Mhaol.*
54. Trans. IV:3, *I would not prefer to be in decorated halls.*
69. Text I:1, more likely *A Flaith, a mhic Dé.*
    The text of V:1 is doubtful.
71. Text I:1, *ar an aoise seo* should more likely be *ar an aois seo.*
    Text I:2, *as taoibh* is doubtful.
    Text II:3, for *sul a dtóirling* read *sul a dtóirling mé* as a possibility.
83. Text I:1, for *i príosún* read *i bpríosún*.
    Text III:3, for *dá ndéanfá* read *dá ndéarfá* as a possibility.
    Text IV:2, for *is tá tathaigh sí uaim* read *atá do thaithíose*

215

uaim as a possibility. This would make the translation as follows: *And I am in the grip of death because of the intensity of my need for your companionship.*

111. Trans. II:2, *and that you cause people to hate me.*

Trans. II:3, for *I shall not give my hand to* — read *I shall not lay my hand on* —

Trans. II:4, for *encouragement* read *proper opportunity.*

Trans. III:2, read *and for one or two other (women) I shall not give her up* as a possibility.

119. Trans. II:2, read *She has no hope again of youth.*

BIBLIOGRAPHY

Only books and collections referred to in this work are included in the Bibliography.

Aird, James, *Aird's Selection of Scotch, English, Irish and Foreign Airs*, adapted to the Fife, Violin, or German Flute, Vols. 1-6 (Glasgow, c.1784-95), see McFadyen below.
Anthologia Hibernica: or monthly collections of science, belles-lettres and history Vols. I-IV (Dublin, 1793/4)
Baring-Gould, Rev. Sabine, and Rev. H. Fleetwood Sheppard, *Garland of Country Song* (London, 1895)
Baring-Gould, Rev. Sabine, and Rev. H. Fleetwood Sheppard, *Songs of the West, Folk Songs of Devon and Cornwall collected from the mouths of the people*, 3rd edition (London n.d. [1905])
Brady, W. Maziere, *The Episcopal Succession in England, Scotland and Ireland A.D. 1400 to 1875*, three volumes (Rome, 1876-77)
Breathnach, Rev. Pádraig, *Songs of the Gael*, four series (Dublin 1915-1922)
Breathnach, Breandán, *Ceol Rinnce na hÉireann* (Dublin, 1963)
Ceol Rinnce na hÉireann, Cuid 2 (Dublin, 1976)
Bryson, J., *A Curious Selection of Favourite Tunes with Variations to which is added fifty Favourite Irish Airs* (Edinburgh, c.1790)
Bunting, Edward, *A General Collection of the Ancient Irish Music*, (London, [1796])
A General Collection of the Ancient Music of Ireland, (London, 1809)
The Ancient Music of Ireland, Arranged for Piano Forte, (Dublin, 1840)
The Ancient Music of Ireland, an edition comprising the three collections by Edward Bunting originally published in [1796] , 1809 and 1840 (Dublin: Walton, 1969)*
Burk, Thomoth, *Twelve English and Twelve Irish Airs* (London, c.1745-50)
Twelve Scotch and Twelve Irish Airs (London, c.1745-50)
Castlehaven (James Touchet, Earl of), *The Earl of Castlehaven's Memoirs* (Dublin 1815) Original edition, London, 1680
Ceol, 'Journal of Irish Music' Vol. 1 No. I (Dublin, 1963; in progress), edited by Breandán Breathnach
Chappell, William, *Popular Music of the Olden Time*, two volumes (New York, 1965)
The Citizen or Native Music of Ireland, (Dublin, 1842)
Cláirseach na nGaedhal, parts I-V (Dublin, 1901-8)
Coffey, Charles, *The Beggar's Wedding*, fourth edition (London 1731)
[Collection of Carolan Tunes] (Dublin? post [1743])
The Complete Peerage (London, 1932 edition)
Connellan, Thaddeus, *An Duanaire (Fonna Seanma)* (Dublin, 1829)
Cooke, B., *Cooke's Selection of Twenty-one Favourite Original Irish Airs (never before printed)* (Dublin, 1793)
Costello, E., *Amhráin Mhuighe Seóla*, issued as Vol. XVI of the *Journal of the Irish Folk Song Society* (London, 1919)

---

* I am grateful to Dr. Brian Boydell for bringing to my attention, after this work had gone to press, new evidence which suggests 1797 as a more likely date for Bunting's first collection.

Crofton, Henry Thomas, *Crofton Memoirs* (York, 1911)
Croker, Crofton, *Researches in the South of Ireland*, (London, 1824)
Crosby, B., *Crosby's Irish Musical Repository* (London, 1808)
Dean-Smith, Margaret, *A Guide to English Folk Song Collections* (Liverpool, 1954)
Dineen, Rev. Patrick S., *Filí na Maighe* (Dublin, 1906)
Amhráin Eoghain Ruaidh Uí Shúilleabháin (Dublin, 1901; 2nd edition, 1923)
Foclóir Gaedhilge agus Béarla/An Irish-English Dictionary (Dublin 1927; new edition, Dublin 1934)
Durfey, Thomas, *Wit and Mirth: or Pills to Purge Melancholy* (London, Vols. I-VI, 1698-1720)
Éigse: A Journal of Irish Studies (Dublin, 1939: in progress)
Fáinne an Lae, weekly paper of the Gaelic League, Dublin, January 1898 to July 1900 after which it was incorporated with *An Claidheamh Soluis*
Feis Ceoil Collection, edited by Arthur Darley and P.J. McCall (Dublin, 1914)
Flood, W.H. Grattan, *A History of Irish Music* (Dublin, 1905)
Fox, Charlotte Milligan, *Annals of the Irish Harpers* (London, 1911)
Galwey, Honoria, *Old Irish Croonauns and other tunes* (London, 1911)
Gibbon, Skeffington, *The Recollections of S. Gibbon* (Dublin, 1829)
Goblet, Y.M. ed., *A Topographical Index of the Parishes and Townlands of Ireland* (Dublin, 1932)
Hannagan, M. and S. Clandillon, *Londubh an Chairn* (Oxford, 1927)
Hardebeck, Carl G., *Seóda Ceoil*, Part I (Belfast, 1908), Parts II and III (Dublin, n.d.)
Hardiman, James, *Irish Minstrelsy*, two volumes (London, 1831)
Henry, Sam, *Songs of the People* Vols, I-III (Coleraine, n.d. [1941]). see also *Songs of the People: Selections from the Sam Henry Collection*, part one, edited by John Moulden (Belfast, 1979)
Herd, David, *Ancient and Modern Scottish Songs*, two volumes (Glasgow, 1869)
Hime's Pocket Book for the German Flute or Violin, Vols. I-VI (Dublin, c.1810)
Hogan, Edmund, *Onomasticon Goedelicum locorum et tribuum Hiberniae et Scotiae* (Dublin, 1910)
Holden, S., *Collection of Old-Established Irish Slow and Quick Tunes* Books I and II (Dublin 1806-7)
Collection of the Most Esteemed Old Irish Melodies, Books I and II (Dublin, post 1806)
Hyde, Douglas, *Abhráin Ghradha Chúige Chonnacht/Love Songs of Connacht* (Dublin and London, 1893)
A Literary History of Ireland (London, 1899)
Irish Folk Music Studies/Éigse Cheol Tíre, Journal of the Folk Music Society of Ireland (Cumann Cheol Tíre Éireann), edited by Hugh Shields, Seoirse Bodley and Breandán Breathnach (Dublin, Vol. I, 1972; Vol. II, 1976; Vol. III, 1981; in progress)
Journal of the Folk Song Society, Vols. I-VIII (London, 1899-1931)
Journal of the Irish Folk Song Society, Vols. I-XXIX (London, 1904-37)
Joyce, P.W., *'Ancient Music of Ireland'* (Dublin, 1873)
Irish Music and Song (Dublin, 1888)
Old Irish Folk Music and Songs (Dublin and London, 1909)
Kennedy, Peter, Ed., *Folksongs of Britain and Ireland* (London, 1975)
Kidson, Frank, *Traditional Tunes* (Oxford, 1891)
Kidson, Frank and Alfred Moffatt, *A Garland of English Folk Songs* (London, 1926)

Kinlock's One Hundred Airs (principally Irish) (Newcastle, c.1815)

Lee, Edmund, *Jackson's Celebrated Irish Tunes* (Dublin, 1774)

Lee, John, *A Favourite Collection of the so much admired Irish Tunes, the original and genuine compositions of Carolan, the celebrated Irish Bard* (Dublin, 1780)

Levey, R.M., *The Dance Music of Ireland*, Vol. I (London, 1858), Vol. II (London, 1873)

Lloyd, A.L., *Folk Song in England* (London 1967)

Lloyd, J.H. *Duanaire na Midhe* (Dublin, 1914)

Milligan-Fox, C., *Four Irish Songs* (Dublin, n.d. [1906?]);

Mitchell, Pat, *The Dance Music of Willy Clancy* (Dublin and Cork, 1976)

Moeran, E.J., *Six Suffolk Songs* (London, 1932)

Moffat, Alfred, *The Minstrelsy of Ireland* (London, 1898)

Mooney, Thomas, *History of Ireland* (Boston, 1846)

Moore, Thomas, *Irish Melodies*, ten numbers and a supplement (Dublin and London, 1807-34)

Morton, Robin, *Folksongs Sung in Ulster* (Cork, 1970)

Mulholland, John, *Collection of Ancient Irish Airs*, Vols. I and II (Belfast, 1810)

Murphy, John, *Collection of Irish Airs and Jiggs* (Paisley, 1809)

MacBean, L., *Songs and Hymns of the Gael* (Stirling, 1900)

MacColuim, Fionán, *Cosa Buidhe Árda* Books I and II (Dublin 1922 and 1924)

McFadden, John, *The Repositary of Scots and Irish Airs Strathspeys and Reels* (Glasgow, c.1795)

McFadyen, J., *A Selection of Scotch, English, Irish and Foreign Airs*, adapted for the Fife, Violin, or German Flute, Vol. 1-6 (Glasgow, c.1784-95), see Aird above

Mac-Geoghegan, James, Abbe, *The History of Ireland*, translated from the French by Patrick O'Kelly (Dublin, 1849)

McGibbon, William, *Scots Tunes*, Bk. II (Edinburgh, 1746)

McGown, *The Repository of Scots and Irish Airs* (Glasgow, c.1800)

Neale, John and William, *A Collection of the Most Celebrated Irish Tunes proper for the Violin, German Flute or Hautboy* (Dublin, c.1726)

Ní Ógáin, *Duanaire Gaedhlge*, three volumes (Dublin, 1921, 1924, 1930)

Ó Baoighill, Seán, *Cnuasacht de Cheoltaí Uladh* (Belfast, 1944)

O'Boyle, Seán, *The Irish Song Tradition* (Dublin, 1977)

Ó Buachalla, Breandán, *Cathal Buí* (Dublin 1975)

O'Daly, John, *The Poets and Poetry of Munster* (Dublin, 1849), second series (Dublin, 1860)

The Irish Language Miscellany (Dublin, 1876)

O'Farrell, *O'Farrell's Collection of National Irish Music for the Union Pipes* (London, c.1797-1800)

O'Farrell's Pocket Companion for the Irish or Union Pipes (London, c.1801-1810)

Ó Flannghaile, Tomás, *Seacht Sárdhánta Gaedhilge* (Dublin, 1908)

Ó Lochlainn, Colm, *More Irish Street Ballads* (Dublin, 1965)

Ó Máille, Tomás, *Amhráin Cearbhalláin* (London, 1916)

Ó Muirgheasa, Énrí, *Dhá Chéad de Cheoltaibh Uladh* (Dublin, 1934)

O'Neill, Francis, Capt., *The Music of Ireland* (Chicago, 1903)

The Dance Music of Ireland (Chicago, 1907)

Irish Folk Music (Chicago, 1910)

Irish Minstrels and Musicians (Chicago, 1913)

O'Rorke, Terence, *History, Antiquities and present state of the parishes of*

Ballysadare and Killvarnet in the county of Sligo (Dublin, 1878)

O'Sullivan, Donal, *The Bunting Collection of Irish Folk Music and Songs*, issued in six parts as Volumes XXII to XXIX of the *Journal of the Irish Folk Song Society* (London, 1927-1939)

Carolan, The Life Times and Music of an Irish Harper, two volumes (London, 1958). Volume II, pp.143-183 contains an edition of 'The Memoirs of Arthur O'Neill'

Songs of the Irish (Dublin, 1960), reprint (Dublin and Cork, 1981)

Oswald, James, *The Caledonian Pocket Companion*, Books I-XII (London, c.1760)

Petrie, George, *Ancient Music of Ireland* (Dublin, 1855)

Music of Ireland (Dublin, 1882)

Roche, Francis, *Collection of Irish Airs, Marches and Dance Tunes*, two volumes (Dublin, 1911); second edition, three volumes (Dublin 1927); new edition in one volume entitled *The Roche Collection of Traditional Irish Music* (Cork: Ossian Publications, 1983)

Sharp, Cecil J., *English Folk Carols* (London, 1911)

Simpson, C.M., *The British Broadside Ballad and its Music* (New Jersey, 1966)

Smith, Charles, *The Ancient and Present State of the County and City of Cork*, two volumes (Dublin, 1750)

The Spirit of the Nation, 'Ballads and Songs by the Writers of "The Nation", with Original and Ancient Music' (Dublin, 1846)

Stanford, Charles, *Songs of Old Ireland* (London, 1882) *The Complete Collection of Irish Music as noted by George Petrie* (London, 1902-5)

Thomson, G., *A Select Collection of Original Scottish Airs*, Vols. 1-3 (Edinburgh, 1803), Vol. 4 (Edinburgh 1805)

Thompson, S., A. and P., *The Hibernian Muse* (London, c.1786)

A Topographical Index of the Parishes and Townlands of Ireland, Irish Mss. Commission (Dublin, 1932)

Traynor, Michael, *The English Dialect of Donegal* (Dublin, 1953)

Walker, Joseph, C., *Historical Memories of the Irish Bards* (Dublin, 1786), second edition, two volumes (Dublin, 1818)

Walsh, Edward, *Irish Popular Songs*, first edition (Dublin, 1847), second edition (Dublin, 1883)

Reliques of Irish Jacobite Poetry, bound with *Poets and Poetry of Munster*, see O'Daly above (Dublin, 1860)

Walsh, J., *Compleat Country Dancing Master* (1st edition, London, 1718)

Walsh, Rev. P.A., *Ceol Ár Sínsear* (Dublin, 1920), originally issued in 1913 as *Fuinn na Smól*

Willis, Anne, 'A Critical Edition of Neal's *Celebrated Irish Tunes*' (unpublished dissertation, University College Cork, 1972)

Wright, Daniel, *Aria di Camera* (London c.1730)

Wright's Compleat Collection of Celebrated Country Dances Vol. I (London, c.1735-40)

Zimmermann, *Songs of Irish Rebellion* (Dublin, 1967)

INDEX OF FIRST LINES

BUNTING'S INDEX OF ENGLISH
TITLES AS GIVEN IN THE
COLLECTION OF 1840

223

225

226

BUNTING'S ANCIENT MUSIC OF IRELAND

EDWARD BUNTING